MARY EMMERLING'S
AT HOME IN THE COUNTRY

MARY EMMERLING'S
AT HOME IN
THE COUNTRY

Recipes and Menus for a Year of Entertaining

PHOTOGRAPHS BY JOSHUA GREENE
TEXT BY CAROL AND LARRY SHEEHAN

Clarkson Potter/Publishers
New York

TO SAMANTHA AND JONATHAN,

MY KIDS,

FOR THEIR LOVE, GOOD HUMOR,

AND SUPPORT

AND TO ALL MY GOOD FRIENDS,

FOR LOVING TO COOK

AND ENTERTAIN WITH ME

Published by Clarkson N. Potter, Inc., 201 East 50th Street, New York, New York 10022. Member of the Crown Publishing Group.

CLARKSON POTTER, POTTER, and colophon are trademarks of Clarkson N. Potter, Inc.

Manufactured in Japan

DESIGN BY GINA DAVIS

Library of Congress Cataloging-in-Publication Data

Emmerling, Mary.
[At home in the country]
Mary Emmerling's at home in the country/Mary Emmerling; photographer,
Joshua Greene.
1. Cookbook. 2. Entertaining. I. Title.
TX714.E47 1991
641.5—dc20   90-27001
CIP

ISBN 0-517-57654-6

10 9 8 7 6 5 4 3 2 1

FIRST EDITION

C O N T

E N T S

INTRODUCTION

My year-round retreat in the country is a shingle-style house with open rooms, a big screened porch, and cupboards spilling over with treasures collected across the country over the years. It's a place where I can take in views of garden, sky, and water at every turn, views that change dramatically in every season. My kids, Samantha and Jonathan, and I always camp here every summer, and we invite guests of all ages to become part of our summer family. During the fall, winter, and spring, we return for as many weekends as we can, and especially on holidays. Somehow holidays in the country mean so much that even when we stay in the city, we try to re-create the country feeling.

The secrets of relaxed country-style entertaining are fresh food and a collection of antique dishes, bowls, and pitchers for displaying nature's bounty to the best advantage.

Our stretch of Long Island is blessed with fertile soil, a seaside climate, landscapes neatly quilted with potato fields and vineyards, and endless white sand dune beaches. Summer folk coexist with proud farmers, tradesmen, and artists, and sophisticated shops and galleries alternate with old-fashioned groceries and soda fountains on Main Street. Even with all of these rural pleasures, and even though our house is a handsome one, it's not the location or the house we love so much as it is the memories we have shared here. Simply enjoying life to its fullest is what our home in the country means to us, and this book is our way of sharing those feelings of friendship and celebration with you.

When I was growing up, my father was a career navy officer, and as he took on his assignments in different parts of the country, the family packed up and moved with him. From this experience I learned firsthand the importance of making a home wherever you happen to be—for as long as you happen to be there. I also learned the essentials of my entertaining style today: flexibility, informality, and organization. These basics may not sound very glamorous, but they are the behind-the-scenes secrets to making any event work—and any house a home. Some people think that practicality and beauty can never go hand in hand, but I believe it's just the opposite. Every object in my home, and every meal I put on the table, is meant to be both useful and attractive. Usually, the best solution from the functional point of view is also

the most visually appealing solution.

First and foremost, in every home I've had, I make the most of the antiques, folk art, tools, containers, linens, quilts, and dishware that I have accumulated over the years. I like to be able to see all of these wonderful collections, so I use them to change the scenery in a room or set a special stage for entertaining. Even if it's just the family, I often pull out an antique (not necessarily expensive) serving dish. Since my collectibles are already on display, it's easy to take a platter off the wall or a kitchen shelf and pile on the burgers from the grill. Likewise, a rustic bench may become a buffet table, an inverted wicker basket doubles as a cocktail table, and old fireplace tools create a wall hanging.

Another aspect of versatility that works for living and entertaining is to use all of the interesting spaces a house has to offer. Rather than limiting entertaining to dining room (winter) and deck (summer), I serve a picnic lunch by the garden or the pool, or set out a sit-down dinner on the porch. Whether makeshift or carefully planned, these unexpected settings seem to inspire the best evenings—full of geniality and romance.

Although my friends are often surprised by the ever-changing look at the Emmerling household, the truth is that I am a traditionalist at heart. The American flag flies every Fourth of July—and waves on many other occasions, too—and a turkey can be found in my oven on Thanksgiving morning. Much as I admire originality in food and menus (I experiment with recipes all the time myself), I find that there is nothing more richly satisfying than those inspired by our national and regional customs. Each time we enjoy a traditional meal, we savor not only the taste of the food, but a lifetime of memories triggered by those familiar flavors. The recipes shared in these pages are ones that have particular memories for me.

"Convenience" and "ease of preparation" are my household words when it comes to entertaining. If every meal I cooked were a major production, I would never invite my friends to visit. So I avoid complicated menus and choose dishes that rely for their success on a combination of good fresh ingredients and wonderful seasonings. I have been collecting recipes ever since I learned to cook as a child, and virtually all of the favorites in my spiral notebook allow for some advance preparation. Sometimes I decide to take the time to gather ingredients and go through the steps to make chicken pot pie, for example, but I make the crust in advance and freeze it, and I limit the rest of the meal to a simple salad and a bowl of fruit.

Of all my tricks, getting organized in advance is probably the most reliable. My pantry and refrigerator are always well stocked with impromptu food and drink: jars of domestic caviar and boxes of crackers on the shelves, lemons and limes in the refrigerator, and vodka in the freezer. With a bandanna tied around the neck of a bottle and a few fancy toothpicks, we have an in-

stant party just a few minutes after surprise guests knock at the door. For an undeniably major event, like Thanksgiving or Christmas, I start making lists, stocking up, and cooking as much as a month ahead. I have even set the table the night before the guests arrived!

Finally, if I have learned anything over the course of many family meals and social evenings, it's to try never to lose my sense of humor. Any time a celebration threatens to turn into an ordeal, I take a break and reconsider my plans. Sometimes it's as simple as dropping a dish from a menu and doubling the recipe for another one (it's just as easy to make two servings of pasta for every diner as it is to make one) or buying a juicy berry pie from the local farmstand instead of making my own. We all deserve to enjoy our holidays and even everyday meals—especially the cook. I refuse to sacrifice my own pleasure to impress my guests with my culinary expertise. In the end they eat well and we all have fun in one another's company.

At Home in the Country is about the fun we have had in our country home, gathering with family and friends. The menus travel the seasons from the first week of January, when I settle in to organize my whole year, to the joys of Christmas the next December. The book is my way of sharing some of those favorite times with distant friends, hoping that the ideas for cooking, entertaining, and decorating that gave us such happy evenings will help make your gatherings just as happy, too.

· ·

It goes without saying that guests enjoy themselves best when they are free to make themselves at home. Suitcases and bathrobes go wherever they fall in the guest room, above, *and a selection of tapes suits a range of musical tastes,* below.

· ·

WINTER COMFORTS

I go into hibernation in the country every January. The days are short and nights are long, a perfect time to move into the darker recesses of the house, curl up with my stacks of magazines, and savor memories of the hectic holidays and travel schedules just past. It's a time when I crave the soul-cleansing comforts of fires and candlelight and the flavors of easy-to-make but deeply satisfying meals like Chicken Pot Pie. I hibernate, but I don't vegetate. I use this month to regroup emotionally, catch up on paperwork, and restore some order to my household. The guests have come and gone and nothing is where it belongs, so I tear apart closets and cupboards and get things back the way *I* like them!

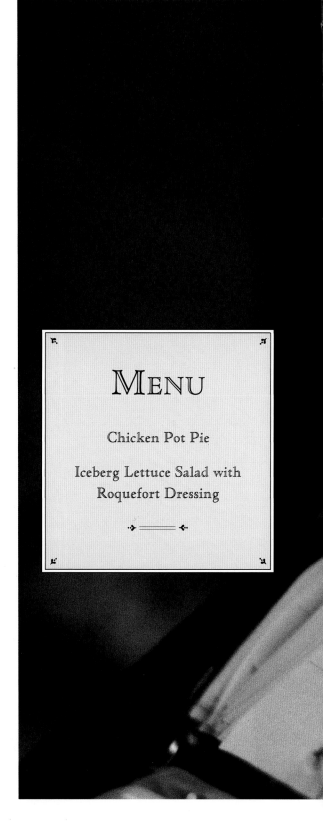

Menu

Chicken Pot Pie

Iceberg Lettuce Salad with
Roquefort Dressing

CHICKEN POT PIE

The key to this recipe is the morel mushrooms, which give an old-fashioned dish a modern twist and a meaty, substantial flavor.

1 to 2 dried morel mushrooms
1 cup dry white wine
1 teaspoon to 2 tablespoons vegetable oil
6 or 7 large boneless, skinless chicken breast halves, cut into bite-size pieces
4 tablespoons (½ stick) unsalted butter
1 pound white mushrooms, washed, stemmed, and quartered
½ cup chopped celery
1 medium yellow onion, chopped
1 teaspoon chopped fresh parsley
¼ cup frozen peas
Salt and pepper
½ cup heavy cream
1 Basic Single Pie Crust (page 93)
White of 1 egg, beaten with 1 teaspoon water until just foamy

Cover the morel mushrooms with the wine and set aside to soak for 1 hour.

Preheat the oven to 400°F.

In a large skillet, heat the oil over medium-high heat. Add the chicken and brown on all sides. Remove the chicken with a slotted spoon; set aside.

Reserving the wine, drain and cut the morels into small pieces. Strain the wine and add it, along with the morels, to the skillet with the chicken drippings. Bring to a boil, scraping the drippings from the bottom of the pan. Add the butter and stir over medium heat until it begins to foam.

Opposite and above: *A savory homecooked meal is the perfect motivation for sitting down with my datebooks, letters, and lists, and starting the new year off on an organized footing.*

Add the white mushrooms, celery, onion, and parsley. Cook over medium heat until the onion is soft and almost translucent.

Add the cooked chicken, peas, and salt and pepper to taste. Add the cream and bring to a boil to reduce slightly. Turn the mixture into a large soufflé dish or casserole.

Cover with the prepared pie crust. Cut out shapes from the remaining bits of pastry and arrange on top. Brush the top of the entire pie with the egg white.

Bake for 35 to 40 minutes, or until the crust is browned and flaky and the chicken mixture is bubbling.

Serves 6–8

Easy to stack and store away

when not in use, rustic twig and wicker trays are perfect for serving food with a flourish, anywhere in the house. Special trays—lined with a colorful cloth napkin —enhance the simplest meal, even a sandwich for one. Colorful outsized platters also double as trays. Whenever I can, I use serving pieces to dress up the kitchen; most of my platters are pretty enough to hang on the wall—for decoration as well as for easy access.

ICEBERG LETTUCE SALAD WITH ROQUEFORT DRESSING

Crisp iceberg lettuce gives just the right contrast to the texture of the pot pie, and the tangy cheese sets off its subtle flavors.

2 heads of iceberg lettuce
3 tablespoons olive oil
2 tablespoons white wine vinegar
¾ to 1 cup crumbled Roquefort
   cheese

    Divide the heads of lettuce into 6 wedges. Place each wedge in a salad bowl.

    Mix the oil and vinegar. Add the crumbled cheese and mix well.

    Pour the dressing over the lettuce wedges and serve.

Serves 6

Winter, as seen across nearby potato fields, right, reduces our range of choices at the market, so I draw on my collections of tableware, left, to brighten our table.

F E B R

U A R Y

CABIN FEVER FARE

The antiques show at the Armory at the end of January brings lots of friends to New York, and I'm always inviting them to spend country weekends with me. Then there's Valentine's Day and the Heart of Country show in Nashville, from which I always come back humming country-western songs. It's only a matter of time before I want a sense of community around our table, but I'm not ready for large-scale entertaining. A dinner of Cornish game hens is something I can shop for in one stop, yet still make festive and appetizing by mixing tin plates, fine china, and Beacon blankets. It was my first editor, Jane West, who told me to "Go west, young woman," and I've been collecting ever since.

Menu

Cornish Game Hens
with Prosciutto and
Cream Cheese

Wild Rice

Snow Peas with Pine Nuts

Angel Food Cake

CORNISH GAME HENS WITH PROSCIUTTO AND CREAM CHEESE

❧

6 Cornish game hens, about
   1 pound each
12 thin slices prosciutto ham,
   about ¼ pound
1½ pounds cream cheese (3 8-ounce
   packages), softened
Salt and pepper
2 tablespoons unsalted butter,
   melted

Preheat the oven to 425°F.

Remove the giblets from the Cornish game hens and discard, or reserve for another use.

Carefully slide 2 slices of the ham between the skin and breast of each bird. Cut each block of cream cheese crosswise in half. Sprinkle salt and pepper to taste on the cream cheese and roll into a ball. Stuff the ball into the cavity of each hen. Truss the hens with butcher's twine, then brush on all sides with the melted butter.

Place hens breast side down in a roasting pan and roast for 10 minutes. Baste the hens and turn them on their sides. Roast for another 10 minutes. Turn onto other side and roast for 10 minutes. Turn them over on their backs, for an additional 15 minutes, or until skin is crispy and juices flow clear when pierced, a total of about 45 minutes.

Serves 6

. . . .

A longhorn key rack, right, *and
dishes worthy of a ranch cookhouse,*
left, *carry out a Western theme
in food and decor.*

SNOW PEAS WITH PINE NUTS

◦↩◦

4 tablespoons olive oil
½ cup pine nuts
1 pound snow peas, stemmed

    In a skillet, heat the oil over medium-high heat. Add the pine nuts and toss until brown. Remove pine nuts and set aside. Add snow peas and sauté, stirring until bright green in color, about 5 minutes. Serve immediately.

Serves 6

A real-life branding iron and a Beacon blanket (serving as a tablecloth) set the scene for a hearty winter meal. Tiny heart-shaped butter pats symbolize February's favorite holiday, left. Snow peas turn a beautiful shade of green when lightly sautéed, above.

AT HOME IN THE COUNTRY

ANGEL FOOD CAKE

When we are having a meal with a rich main course like Cornish Game Hens with Prosciutto and Cream Cheese, I like to serve a light dessert. Angel Food Cake is very satisfying, but it's actually one of the original no-cholesterol treats.

  1 **cup sifted cake flour**
1½ **cups sugar**
 ¼ **teaspoon salt**
Whites of 12 large eggs
1¼ **teaspoons cream of tartar**
1¼ **teaspoons lemon extract**

    Preheat the oven to 375°F.

    Stir the flour with ¾ cup sugar and the salt.

    Beat the egg whites with the cream of tartar until soft peaks form. Add the lemon extract. Add the remaining sugar, 2 tablespoons at a time; beat well after each addition. Sift ¼ cup flour mixture over egg whites; fold in carefully. Fold in remaining flour mixture by fourths. Turn into a 10-inch tube pan.

    Bake 35 to 40 minutes or until a toothpick inserted in the center comes out clean. Invert the tube of the pan over the neck of a bottle; cool completely. Remove from the pan.

Serves 10–12

. . . .

The heart-shaped tube pan is a gift from a friend who appreciates my passion for hearts of all kinds.

MAR

SPRING BREAK SUPPER

March is the time to think spring break. The fireplace is still the blazing focal point of our home life, and winter hours are still the rule. I'll invite four to six friends over—no more, or I wouldn't get the chance to talk to everyone—and I'll make it on the early side, allowing guests to be on their way home at a reasonable hour. The food is out and ready to cook beforehand, so my company can enjoy the appetizing look of the colorful vegetables and the meat marinating in a favorite dish. To set a welcoming mood, I preprogram our tape deck with classical music or the soundtrack from *Out of Africa,* and softly light the room with white candles and groupings of kerosene lamps—a kind of winter safari.

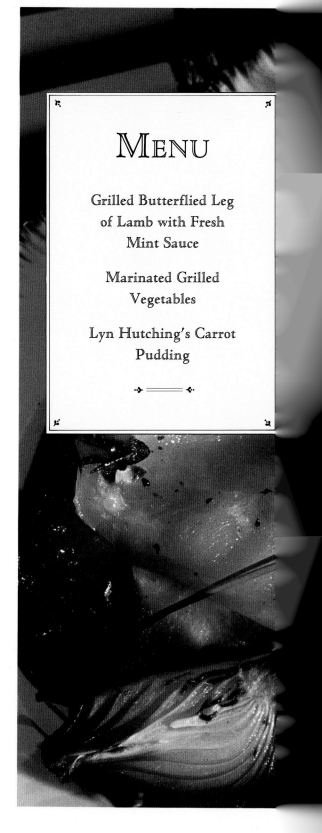

MENU

Grilled Butterflied Leg
of Lamb with Fresh
Mint Sauce

Marinated Grilled
Vegetables

Lyn Hutching's Carrot
Pudding

I hate to let wonderful old things gather dust. That's why I always bring out my favorite antiques for entertaining. I don't worry about accidents that might befall my beloved quilts and other objects. They were all made to serve a useful household function in the first place, and a stain or a frayed edge only adds to their charm. I'm always on the lookout to add to my collections, too, and winter is an especially fruitful time to explore the shops and secondhand stores. I like to collect in well-defined categories—for example, Western items such as tin plates, twig napkin rings, Beacon blankets from the 1920s, and an assortment of old-fashioned kerosene lanterns. Used together, a collection creates a very special atmosphere. But I'm not a slave to "sets" of things. In fact, imperfect matches of plates and dishes can be charming.

GRILLED BUTTERFLIED LEG OF LAMB WITH FRESH MINT SAUCE

1 leg of lamb, about 7 to 8 pounds
1 cup honey
1 cup soy sauce
8 garlic cloves, finely chopped

For the mint sauce:
1 tablespoon superfine sugar
½ cup white wine vinegar
¼ cup minced fresh mint leaves

Have your butcher butterfly the leg of lamb.

Combine the honey, soy sauce, and garlic in a small bowl. Place the lamb in a large roasting pan or shallow baking dish. Pour the marinade over the lamb, cover with plastic wrap, and marinate in the refrigerator for 12 hours or overnight.

To grill outdoors: Oil the grill or a hinged barbecue rack. Prepare the charcoal and, when the coals are white-hot, place the lamb on the grill or rack. Grill for 10 to 15 minutes on each side for rare, watching carefully. Adjust the grilling time according to your taste. Remove the lamb to a platter and allow it to rest 10 minutes before slicing.

To broil indoors: Preheat the broiler. Oil a broiler pan. The cooking time is the same—10 to 15 minutes on each side. Let the meat rest for 10 minutes before carving.

For the mint sauce: Dissolve the sugar in the vinegar. (If the vinegar is highly acidic, dilute it with water.) Pour over the mint in a bowl. Cover and let stand in a warm place for 30 minutes.

Serves 6

. . . .

The most romantic light comes from the fire, kerosene lanterns, and candles, above and right, *setting the mood for grilled lamb,* left.

Some of my friends who say they hate to cook believe that they have to make the fanciest dishes to impress their guests. My philosophy is: If it tastes fresh and delicious, why not keep it simple? If portions of a dinner menu can be prepared beforehand, so much the better. But I never stint on presentation, knowing how much it adds to the fun of a social gathering, and how good it makes a special guest feel. Serving dishes and containers are fun to collect, and they make a real impact at the dinner table.

MARINATED GRILLED VEGETABLES

‏ు‌

If you plan to serve the vegetables with the butterflied leg of lamb, grill the vegetables first and set aside. Serve hot, room temperature, or cold.

- 1 cup olive oil
- 3 medium zucchini, stems removed, halved lengthwise
- 3 medium yellow squash, stems removed, halved lengthwise
- 2 teaspoons salt
- 1 teaspoon black pepper
- 3 red bell peppers
- 3 yellow bell peppers
- 3 green bell peppers
- 2 red Italian peppers
- 3 large yellow onions

Place ½ cup of the olive oil in a small bowl. Using a pastry brush, lightly brush the zucchini and squash slices with the oil. Place the remaining ½ cup olive oil in a large bowl. Add the salt and pepper; set aside.

To grill outdoors: When the coals are hot, roast the peppers and onions whole, turning frequently to avoid burning. When the peppers and onions are soft, remove from the grill and set aside. Grill the zucchini and squash slices until lightly browned on each side. Remove and allow to cool on a tray.

Under cold running water, carefully remove the skins, stems, and seeds from the peppers. Cut the peppers in half and add to the oil in the large bowl. Cut the onions in quarters and add to the peppers. When the zucchini and squash are cool, add to the peppers and onions. Toss to combine well. Cover and set aside until ready to serve, or prepare a day ahead and refrigerate.

To grill indoors: Preheat the broiler and follow instructions for grilling outdoors.

Serves 6

LYN HUTCHING'S CARROT PUDDING

Lyn is the best cook I know. She makes up recipes based on what she thinks will work together. The flavor of this pudding is a lot like that of a carrot quick bread.

  2 pounds carrots, peeled and
     grated
½ cup (1 stick) unsalted butter
Juice of ½ lemon
Salt
¾ cup sugar
Ground ginger
1½ cups heavy cream
  3 large eggs
Black pepper

Preheat the oven to 350°F.

In a saucepan, combine the carrots, butter, lemon juice, salt, sugar, and a dash of ginger. Add just enough water to cover. Bring to a boil, reduce the heat, cover, and simmer for 30 minutes, or until the liquid evaporates.

In a small bowl, combine the cream and eggs, and season with pepper to taste. Stir the sauce into the carrot mixture. Turn into a lightly buttered 1-quart heart-shape pan or 9-inch square pan.

Bake for 35 to 40 minutes, or until pudding is set and top is lightly browned.

Serves 6

. . . .

Attractive vegetable courses, right and opposite above, *can be set out before the main event. Old tools,* left, *hang by the fire.*

R I L

HEARTY APRIL DINNER

I can't imagine a wonderful meal without a friend to share it, and I can't make new friends without eventually finding some way to break bread with them. Restaurateur Christopher Idone introduced me to this country ham recipe one April when he came out to my house for a photo shoot, and now I turn to it every Easter. Both winter and summer swing through spring unpredictably, like pendulums gone awry, and the kids, studying for exams, have tons of homework. A hearty cold-weather menu, served on yelloware evoking the warmer days to come, is a pleasant reward for all of us at the end of a hard-work weekend. To add cheer, I buy fresh tulips or bring out the forced bulbs.

Menu

Cream of Broccoli Soup

Christopher Idone's Baked
Country Ham

Mashed Potatoes

Lemon Mousse with
Blueberries

38

CREAM OF BROCCOLI SOUP

The green of this soup really says "spring." Serve it in white or black bowls to set off the color.

  2 bunches broccoli
⅔ cup unsalted butter
½ cup all-purpose flour
  3 cups milk
  2 cups chicken stock
  2 teaspoons salt
¼ teaspoon white pepper
¼ teaspoon lemon juice
  1 garlic clove, sliced
  1 tablespoon Worcestershire sauce
¼ teaspoon Tabasco
Yolks of 3 large eggs, beaten
  2 cups heavy cream

Wash the broccoli. Trim and dry, reserving a few raw florets for garnish.

Melt the butter in a medium saucepan over medium heat until it stops foaming. Add the broccoli and cook until soft. Blend in the flour and simmer, stirring constantly, until smooth and bubbling. Stir in the milk, stock, salt, white pepper, lemon juice, garlic, Worcestershire sauce, and Tabasco. Reduce the heat to low and continue to cook until the soup begins to thicken, stirring constantly.

Process the soup in blender or food processor. Return the soup to the saucepan. Whisk a little of the hot soup into the egg yolks to warm them. Add the yolks to the saucepan and stir. Add the heavy cream and salt to taste. Serve with the reserved florets as a garnish.

Serves 6

CHRISTOPHER IDONE'S BAKED COUNTRY HAM

❧

1 country-cured ham (about
   12 pounds)

For the glaze:
¼ cup apricot preserves
¼ cup dark brown sugar
1 tablespoon dry mustard
¼ cup bourbon

Place the ham in a large kettle, cover with cold water, and let soak for 24 hours.

Pour off the water. Cover with fresh cold water and bring to a simmer over medium heat. Set aside to cool.

Preheat the oven to 350°F.

Trim away the ham's outer skin, leaving about 4 inches around the bone (remove as little fat as possible). Score, then place on a rack in a roasting pan. Bake about 20 minutes per pound, or 3 hours 40 minutes all together.

For the glaze: Mix the ingredients in a small saucepan over medium heat until the sugar dissolves.

During the last 20 minutes of baking, glaze the ham. Return it to the oven and raise the oven temperature to 450°F.

Transfer the ham to a serving platter. Allow to cool for 15 minutes before carving. Serve with mashed potatoes.

Serves 10–12

. . . .

For a casual supper, soup bowls and dinner plates, opposite, and a large antique platter of sliced ham, right, find room among the books.

LEMON MOUSSE WITH BLUEBERRIES

&

1 quart fresh blueberries, washed and
   cleaned, or frozen blueberries
1 cup sugar
5 large eggs, separated
Juice of 2 large lemons
1 cup heavy cream
2 teaspoons grated lemon peel

Pour the berries into a glass serving bowl and sprinkle with ¼ cup sugar. Cover and refrigerate.

In the top of a glass or stainless steel double boiler, beat the egg yolks with the remaining ¾ cup sugar until the mixture becomes a light lemon color. Add the lemon juice and cook over just simmering water, whisking constantly, until the mixture heavily coats a spoon. Do not boil. Set aside to cool.

Beat the egg whites until stiff but not dry. Fold gently into the lemon mixture.

Whip the heavy cream; fold into the egg mixture with the grated lemon peel. Cover and chill well. To serve, spoon the mousse over the berries.

Serves 6–8

Lemon and blueberries, left and above, are a zesty combination for a spring dessert.

TASTE OF SUMMER

This is the month we've all been waiting for, when we begin to shift our seasonal gears and start enjoying such classic summer treats as swordfish on the grill—even if the cook has to wear a sweater to do the grilling! It's the time I roll up my winter rugs and brighten the house with straw mats and rag rugs. We dust off all the outdoor furniture, as well as any chair or table or bench I might have acquired on my antiquing trails over the winter. It's fun to find new ways to use furniture for entertaining in different areas in the yard or on the porch. The small touches—special furniture, folk art, and table settings—are what make the garden into an outdoor dining room for all but the rainiest weather.

MENU

Grilled Swordfish

Zucchini Boats

Broiled Tomatoes

Mother's Sour Cream Cake

GRILLED SWORDFISH

❧

In the spring I am always in the garden, planting flowers and herbs. Dill is one I love (so do the rabbits), so this grilled swordfish dinner is a May must. We grill outdoors in any weather—except blizzards!

  2 **bunches fresh dill, finely chopped**
¼ **cup olive oil**
  4 **garlic cloves, finely chopped**
Salt and pepper
  3 **large swordfish steaks, about**
    ¾ **inch thick**

Prepare a charcoal grill or the broiler. If using the grill, heat the coals to white-hot.

In a bowl, combine the dill, olive oil, garlic, and salt and pepper. Spread the sides of each swordfish steak with marinade and place in a dish. Cover and refrigerate for 20 minutes.

Remove the swordfish from the dish and reserve the marinade. Place on the grill or under the broiler and baste with the marinade. Grill 5 minutes. With a spatula, carefully flip the steaks over, baste with the remainder of the marinade, and grill for another 5 minutes.

Flip over again and grill for another minute, just to brown the marinade on that side. (Be careful not to overcook.) Serve at once.

Serves 6

. . . .

Fragrant topiaries, above right, a straw hat, right, and out-of-season corn, opposite, are elements of a "we-can't-wait-for-spring" evening.

ZUCCHINI BOATS

❧

This makes a great appetizer, too, but we serve it as a side dish.

  4 **large zucchini, stems removed**
  1 **cup sour cream**
  1 **medium red onion, finely**
    chopped
Salt and pepper
¼ **to ½ cup grated Parmesan cheese**

Preheat the oven to 350°F.

Steam the zucchini or parboil until tender, about 3 to 5 minutes. Let cool a bit, split lengthwise, and scoop out the seeds.

Mix the sour cream, onion, and salt and pepper to taste.

Fill the zucchini boats with the sour cream mixture and sprinkle generously with Parmesan cheese.

Bake until browned, about 10 to 15 minutes. Serve at once.

Serves 8

I love floppy old sun hats. I line them up on peg racks, along with a variety of equally venerable baseball caps, ready for guests and family alike. A few hats never make it back at the end of the season, but friends leave others behind. In winter, they hang on the wall like a portrait of summers past.

BROILED TOMATOES

8 ripe beefsteak tomatoes
8 garlic cloves, each cut into
   4 slivers
4 tablespoons fresh thyme leaves
4 tablespoons olive oil
Salt and pepper

Preheat the broiler.

Cut each tomato in half horizontally. Place the tomatoes, cut sides up, in a baking dish large enough to hold them.

Insert 2 slivers of garlic into the top of each tomato. Sprinkle with the thyme, olive oil, and salt and pepper to taste.

Broil for about 5 minutes, until the tops brown.

Serves 8

MOTHER'S SOUR CREAM CAKE

We grew up in Rehoboth Beach, Delaware, as kids. For Mother's Day we always cooked Mom her favorite cake. Now I always hope my kids will make it for me.

1½ cups (3 sticks) unsalted butter,
    at room temperature
 3 cups granulated sugar
 6 large eggs, separated
 3 cups sifted all-purpose flour
¼ teaspoon baking soda
 1 cup sour cream
 2 tablespoons vanilla extract
Superfine sugar

Preheat the oven to 325°F. Butter a bundt pan.

Using a mixer, beat the butter with the granulated sugar until fluffy. Beat the egg yolks and blend well into the butter mixture.

Sift the flour with the baking soda. Add the dry ingredients to the butter-egg mixture alternately with the sour cream and vanilla.

Beat the egg whites until stiff but not dry. Fold the whites into the cake batter. Turn the batter into the buttered pan.

Bake for 1½ hours, until a toothpick or tester inserted in the center comes out clean. Sprinkle on superfine sugar. Cool in the pan.

Serves 8–10

. . . .

Spring welcomes visitors in many cherished forms in the countryside, left and opposite, *while an ironstone cake stand,* above, *puts a favorite family recipe on its own pedestal.*

POPOVERS FOR MOM

I can hear them from my bedroom in the morning, Samantha and Jonathan whispering about how to do my eggs and what tray to use and how many popovers Mom is likely to eat this Mother's Day. My children's arrival at bedside with their special breakfast for me, complete with Mother's Day cards of their own creation, is a treat that never fails to please. I once put the kids through "cooking school," believing it's a good idea for all youngsters to know how to prepare a simple meal, set a table, and clean up afterward. When they're out in "the real world," I know they'll get along that much better. The pampering I receive at Mother's Day is an unexpected dividend of their kitchen skills.

MENU

Mother's Favorite Eggs

Jonathan's Popovers

Cranberry Juice with Seltzer

JONATHAN'S POPOVERS

I could eat my son's popovers every day of the year, but on Mother's Day they are truly the best. Don't wait once they're out of the oven—the secret is to pop them in your mouth as soon as they are cool enough to load with butter and jam.

2 large eggs
¾ cup milk
2 tablespoons unsalted butter or margarine, melted
¾ cup sifted all-purpose flour
Vegetable shortening

Preheat the oven to 375°F.

Place a cast-iron popover pan or 8 custard cups on a baking sheet and set in the oven to preheat.

In a medium bowl, beat the eggs until frothy. Beat in the milk and butter. Fold in the flour, 2 tablespoons at a time.

Carefully remove the hot popover pan from the oven and grease with vegetable shortening. Divide the batter evenly among the popover cups.

Bake the popovers for 35 to 40 minutes, or until puffed and firm on top. Serve immediately with butter and jam.

Serves 4

. . . .

An oversized platter used as a tray and a handmade card for Mom make breakfast in bed into a festive celebration.

The curative powers of the bath have been understood since ancient times. The country bathroom is well stocked with warm robes, fresh towels, pampering scents and oils, and a humidity-loving orchid as a touch of elegance.

OLD FAVORITES

My former roommate, Judy, is responsible for one of my most durable recipes, a lasagne that diners of all ages have relished at my home. In the spring, when I'm eager to get out into the garden, a do-ahead dish like this can be a godsend. By now my mints, planted around the outdoor shower, have just pushed through the ground and soon will be full of foliage. I remember the same usage of mint plants for their natural perfumes from our cottage in Rehoboth on the Delaware shore, when I was a girl. And I love floral napkins because they remind me of my grandmother's redolent rose garden in Georgetown. So many good ideas for decorating and entertaining come from childhood memories.

MENU

Judy Scanlon's Lasagne

Spinach Salad

Carol Glasser's Custard

For Samantha, above, *introduced to cooking early, kitchen chores are fun, not drudgery. Framed flying boots,* right, *rest on a ladderback chair.*

Photographs, paintings, and drawings are so important to me that I exhibit them in as many ways as possible. Mounted or not, framed or unframed, they hang on walls, rest on small easels atop tables, or just lean on the back of a chair, a desktop, or a fireplace mantel. Pictures can even become a changing gallery—lined up along a shelf or hallway floor, overlapping a little, they tempt the visitor to pick them up and look a little closer.

JUDY SCANLON'S LASAGNE

1 pound lasagne noodles
3 pounds ground beef
1 quart homemade spaghetti sauce, or 2 large (32-ounce) jars of your favorite pasta sauce
1 pound cottage cheese
1 cup shredded mozzarella
Salt and pepper

Preheat the oven to 325°F.

Cook the noodles in rapidly boiling water until just tender.

Brown the beef in a skillet. Drain off excess fat. Add the pasta sauce to the beef and stir. Spoon a thin layer of sauce in a lasagne pan. Add a layer of noodles and top with cottage cheese and mozzarella. Add a layer of sauce. Add more layers of sauce, noodles, and cheese, ending with a layer of noodles brushed with sauce.

Bake 25 minutes until top is brown and sauce is bubbling. Let stand for 5 to 10 minutes before serving.

Serves 6–8

SPINACH SALAD

1 pound fresh spinach
Salt (optional)
1 garlic clove, peeled
2 tablespoons lemon juice
6 tablespoons olive oil
Freshly ground black pepper
2 hard-cooked eggs, cut into wedges
½ medium red onion, sliced thin

Wash the spinach well in several changes of clear water. Cut away stems and discard. Drain spinach leaves and chill in a damp, clean cloth or paper towels. Tear into bite-size pieces.

Sprinkle the bottom of a salad bowl with salt and rub with garlic. Add the lemon juice and olive oil and chill the bowl. When ready to serve, add the spinach and sprinkle with pepper. Garnish with egg wedges and onion rings and toss lightly with a fork and spoon.

Serves 4–6

CAROL GLASSER'S CUSTARD

Custard strikes fear into the hearts of some cooks, but Carol's recipe is foolproof. You can double the recipe but use the same amount of sugar if you don't like it too sweet.

2 large eggs, beaten
4 cups half-and-half
⅔ cup sugar
2 tablespoons cornstarch
2 tablespoons vanilla extract
Mint leaves, berries, or nutmeg

Combine all ingredients except garnish in a saucepan and stir over low heat for approximately 5 minutes or until the custard coats the back of a wooden spoon.

Pour into custard cups. Refrigerate until set, about 2 hours. Garnish with mint or berries or sprinkle with nutmeg.

Serves 4

J U

SUMMER APPETIZERS

This time of year, especially in beach communities, friends begin to drop in unexpectedly to renew acquaintances, to celebrate the good weather, or just to gossip. My pantry is always ready for a party, stocked ahead of time with a few favorite basics like cheeses, caviar (grocery-store variety), dried fruit, and heart-shaped crackers. Then it's easy enough, a few days before the weekend, to stop by the vegetable stand and make a simple vinaigrette and foolproof dips that will keep. Collections of antique containers and utensils make an imaginative offering of simple fare, proving once again that food doesn't have to be complicated to be delicious, and entertaining need not be fancy or difficult to be fun.

MENU

Caviar Pie

Crudités (Cucumbers, Red and Yellow Peppers, Green and Purple String Beans)

Broiled New Potatoes with Garlic Mayonnaise

Cheese Board (Stilton, Cheddar, Brie, and Heart Crackers)

Sandy Horvitz's Dip

Barbara Ohrbach's Summer Dip

62

CAVIAR PIE

8 hard-cooked eggs, finely
  chopped
1 medium onion, finely chopped
6 tablespoons (¾ stick) unsalted
  butter, melted
White pepper
¾ cup sour cream
9 ounces (about 1¼ cups) lumpfish
  caviar
2 lemons, each cut into 8 wedges
16 slices thin white bread, cut with
  a small heart cookie cutter and
  toasted in a 250° F. oven for 10
  to 15 minutes

In a medium bowl, combine the
hard-cooked eggs, onion, butter,
white pepper to taste, and ¼ cup of
the sour cream. Spread the mixture
in a 9-inch pie plate. Spread the remaining ½ cup sour cream on top.
Cover and chill for at least 3 hours,
or overnight.

Spread the caviar evenly over
the sour cream and serve the caviar
pie, cut into wedges, with the lemon
wedges and toast hearts.

Serves many

*Crudités, left, and the pièce de
résistance Caviar Pie, above, are the
mainstays of the cocktail party.*

BROILED NEW POTATOES WITH GARLIC MAYONNAISE

1 pound small new potatoes (the
   smaller the better)
1 tablespoon olive oil
½ teaspoon fresh thyme leaves,
   stripped from the stems
Coarsely ground pepper

For the garlic mayonnaise:
 6 to 8 garlic cloves, peeled
 1 cup mayonnaise
 ½ cup plain yogurt

Preheat the broiler.

In a bowl, toss together all the ingredients to coat the potatoes.

Place the potatoes on a baking sheet and broil until cooked through, about 15 minutes. Toss with a spoon from time to time.

For the garlic mayonnaise: Under the broiler, roast the garlic until browned outside and soft inside. Crush the garlic with the side of a wide-blade knife. Add to the mayonnaise and yogurt and mix well.

Cover and refrigerate overnight or for a week.

Serves 6

Additional appetizing treats are tiny new potatoes, above, *and tempting cheeses,* right.

SANDY HORVITZ'S DIP

Yolks of 6 large eggs
⅓ cup orange-flavored mustard
  (Sandy uses Silver Palate
  orange mustard)
⅓ cup red wine vinegar
⅓ cup soy sauce
½ cup Oriental (dark) sesame oil
4½ cups corn oil

Blend the egg yolks and mustard in a food processor or blender. Add the remaining ingredients and mix well. Serve with crudités and toast hearts. Keeps in the refrigerator for a week.

Makes 6–7 cups

. . . .

Summer is made for antiquing, **left and above,** *especially in the all-American convertible with Star in the front seat, and aerodynamic toothpicks,* **opposite left,** *for eating fresh hors d'oeuvres afterward.*

BARBARA OHRBACH'S SUMMER DIP

Barbara Ohrbach (author of The Scented Room) has a special touch in the garden. I really like the way she uses fresh herbs, as she does in this summer dip.

¾ cup mayonnaise
¾ cup sour cream
⅓ cup chopped fresh parsley
3 tablespoons finely chopped chives
1 garlic clove, crushed
1 tablespoon white wine vinegar
¼ teaspoon pepper
⅛ teaspoon salt

Combine all the ingredients and mix well. Cover and refrigerate overnight. Serve with crudités and toast hearts. Keeps in the refrigerator for weeks.

Makes 1¾ cups

THE BREAKFAST CLUB

In a busy social season, especially during the "people month" of June, it's sometimes easy to lose touch with the people you cherish the most. I like to take advantage of the natural serenity of a Sunday morning to catch up with the family over breakfast. It's really the best time to get everybody together, especially with kids following their summer instincts to pursue activities in all directions. We'll all pitch in to cook up a batch of sugary French toast, and if it is sunny I'll dress up a table outdoors with my cheeriest linens. When all is quiet and slow-moving, we see what wonders nature has worked in the garden and give one another the luxury of time, communication, and understanding in a favorite place.

MENU

French Toast with
Berry Puree

Bacon

Fresh Orange Juice

Coffee

FRENCH TOAST WITH BERRY PUREE

It's still hard to get the kids to eat breakfast, but they never refuse this classic. I can't resist it either.

2 large eggs
½ cup milk
¼ teaspoon ground cinnamon
⅛ teaspoon ground nutmeg
½ teaspoon vanilla extract
6 to 8 slices thin white bread

For the berry puree:
1 pint blueberries, raspberries, or
  strawberries
Sugar (optional)

Whisk together the eggs, milk, cinnamon, nutmeg, and vanilla. Soak the bread slices in the egg mixture until saturated. Fry in a hot skillet until cooked through, about 5 minutes on each side.

For the berry puree: Wash the berries. Add optional sugar as desired, and puree for several seconds in a blender or food processor.

Serves 2–3

. . . .

A hearty outdoor breakfast, **left,** *fuels a day's work in the garden,* **right,** *a favorite activity at this time of year. By late June the perennials in the herb garden start to come into flower, thanks in part, perhaps, to the good-luck value of our traditional bee skep. Eating outside has only one drawback: the family gardener keeps sneaking away from the table to pluck an offending weed.*

A POOLSIDE PICNIC

For me the whole point of summer is hanging out at the beach with my family and friends. I could spend every day swimming and sitting on a blanket in the sand when the weather is good—and even when it isn't. The Fourth of July is the best day of the summer and one of my favorite holidays—we raise the flags and pack a picnic. Sometimes the picnic is so elaborate that we get no farther than the pool, but that means we can have ice cream with our brownies and eat our barbecued chicken fresh from the grill. Because this is a traditional get-together, I use recipes collected over the years. Not only are they great, personally tested dishes, but the memories associated with them add flavor to the meal.

MENU

Charley Gold's Grilled
Shrimp

Lyn Hutching's Corn Salad

Barbecued Chicken with
Dad's Barbecue Sauce

Fruit Salad with Fresh
Cream

Barbara Brook's Brownies

Hot Fudge Sauce for
Ice Cream

Mother's Chocolate Cake

Old-Fashioned Lemonade

I approach "furnishing" yard and garden the same
way I do the house. After all, it is a living space, especially in the
warm-weather months, and I like to have enough comforts to
encourage friends and family to feel right at home. Old benches make
useful serving tables or gardening sheds, or just a great place to stretch
out. Flea-market sports equipment is all we need to satisfy most of our
visiting weekend athletes. And I'm always on the lookout for
lighthearted folk art for the garden, where in my opinion a sense of
humor is sometimes lacking but never out of place.

CHARLEY GOLD'S GRILLED SHRIMP

If you make this on the same grill as the Barbecued Chicken with Dad's Barbecue Sauce, grill the shrimp first and enjoy as an appetizer while the chicken barbecues.

2 pounds jumbo shrimp
¼ cup soy sauce
3 garlic cloves
1-inch piece fresh ginger, peeled and
    finely chopped
Grated zest of 1 lemon
¼ cup olive oil
1 cup orange juice
4 tablespoons sugar

Peel and clean the shrimp.

Combine all the other ingredients in a small bowl. Place the shrimp in a glass or crockery bowl, pour the marinade over the shrimp, and refrigerate for 1 hour or more.

Meanwhile, soak bamboo skewers in water and prepare the grill. When the coals are white-hot, place the shrimp on the skewers and then onto the grill, reserving the marinade. Grill the shrimp about 2 minutes on each side, just until they curl and turn pink inside, brushing frequently with the marinade.

Serves 6

. . . .

I love everything that comes off a hot grill. When the meal is a simple one, even the family barbecue chef (my brother, Terry, opposite above) has time to relax before grilling the shrimp, **right.**

LYN HUTCHING'S CORN SALAD

Lyn's recipes always work. She has a great way with vegetables. See her Carrot Pudding and her BLT Salad, pages 35 and 99.

½ teaspoon sugar
16 ounces corn kernels (1 large bag)
 1 large red bell pepper, diced
 1 or 2 large green bell peppers, diced
 1 medium Bermuda onion, thinly sliced
 8 ounces Monterey Jack cheese, diced
 1 tablespoon olive oil
Ground cumin
Salt and pepper
Cayenne pepper

Put an inch or two of water in a medium saucepan, add the sugar, and bring to a boil. Add the corn, return to a boil, and cook about 5 minutes, until heated. Drain and cool under cold running water. Pat dry with paper towels.

Add the red and green bell peppers, onion, and cheese; toss well. Add the oil and toss to coat. Season with cumin, salt, pepper, and cayenne to taste.

Serve at room temperature.

Serves 6

BARBECUED CHICKEN WITH DAD'S BARBECUE SAUCE

❧

2 chickens, 2½ to 3 pounds each
1 cup (2 sticks) unsalted butter
½ cup catsup
1 tablespoon sugar
1½ teaspoons lemon juice
1 tablespoon Worcestershire sauce
1 garlic clove, pressed
1 small onion, finely chopped
¼ teaspoon Tabasco
Salt and pepper

Prepare the grill and light the charcoal.

Combine all the ingredients except the chicken in a medium glass or stainless steel saucepan. Simmer, covered, over low heat for 5 minutes.

When the coals are white-hot, place chickens on grill, and baste with sauce every 3 minutes. Turn after 20 minutes and grill for another 20 minutes.

Serves 6

Fresh-cut grass, corn so tender it cooks in seconds, succulent watermelon, and chicken barbecuing on a grill—those elements of summer blend together for me in a feast of my childhood senses. I use my gayest spongeware, opposite, to hold a friend's colorful corn salad.

. . . .

BARBARA BROOK'S BROWNIES

✦

4 ounces unsweetened chocolate
1 cup (2 sticks) unsalted butter
2 cups sugar
1 tablespoon vanilla extract
4 large eggs, lightly beaten
1 cup sifted all-purpose flour

Preheat the oven to 325°F.

Melt the chocolate with the butter in the top of a double boiler set over barely simmering water. Remove from the heat. Stir in the sugar and vanilla, then the beaten eggs and flour. Mix well.

Spread in a 9-inch square greased and floured baking pan. Bake for 25 to 30 minutes. It's okay if the center is a bit gooey, so long as the batter is hot all the way through.

Serves 8–10

HOT FUDGE SAUCE FOR ICE CREAM

✦

4 ounces unsweetened chocolate
½ cup (1 stick) unsalted butter
1½ cups evaporated milk
3 cups sugar
½ teaspoon salt
2 teaspoons vanilla extract

In the top of a double boiler set over barely simmering water, melt the chocolate and the butter, stirring occasionally. Add the evaporated milk, sugar, and salt, and cook, stirring occasionally, for 20 minutes.

Stir in the vanilla; transfer the sauce to a bowl. The sauce keeps, covered and chilled, for up to 2 weeks. To serve, reheat the sauce in the top of a double boiler set over barely simmering water.

Makes about 3½ cups

Fresh lemons clustered in a wire egg basket are destined for summer's favorite beverage.

. . . .

OLD-FASHIONED LEMONADE

✦

Pile lots of ice cubes in a gallon jug, mason jar, or thermos—something big and festive. Slice and squeeze in 12 fresh lemons, adding the rinds to the juice. Stir in sugar to taste and add just enough water to fill the jug.

Serves 6, with refills

The picnic basket is always set to go with dishes and linens.

MOTHER'S CHOCOLATE CAKE

❧

Chocolate lovers will heap their plates with this rich cake, along with Barbara Brook's Brownies and Ice Cream with Hot Fudge Sauce.

½ cup (1 stick) unsalted butter or margarine
2 cups sugar
3 large eggs
3 ounces unsweetened chocolate, melted and cooled
1½ teaspoons vanilla extract
2 cups sifted cake flour
2 teaspoons baking soda
½ teaspoon salt
1 cup sour cream
1 4-ounce package instant chocolate pudding mix
½ cup milk

Preheat the oven to 350°F., and grease and flour an 8-inch spring-form pan.

Beat together the butter and sugar in a large bowl. Add the eggs and beat until light and fluffy. Beat in the chocolate and vanilla.

Sift together the flour, baking soda, and salt. Add the dry ingredients to the butter-and-egg mixture, alternately with the sour cream, pudding mix, and butter mixture. Stir in the milk to thin the batter.

Pour batter into the pan and bake for 50 to 55 minutes or until cake tests done. Cool in the pan on a wire rack for 10 minutes. Turn out onto a rack, and cool completely. Fill or frost as desired.

Serves 8

Our cake is dressed up for the Fourth, with stars dusted with powdered sugar, above.

FAMILY BEACH PARTY

Give me a sandy beach, a classic land yacht like my brother Terry's Bonneville convertible, a camera loaded with film, and a portable feast of cold roast chicken, potato salad, deviled eggs, and fruit pie—that's the essence of the American summertime to me. I make plenty for the picnic, because I know how good the leftovers will taste the next day—and I get a cook's day off in the process. I'm not a serious photographer, but I love to record the good times with friends and family in hundreds of snapshots, which I toss willy-nilly into a big platter or bowl back at the house. Then when winter rolls around, I sort through the memories and experience the warming pleasures of summer all over again.

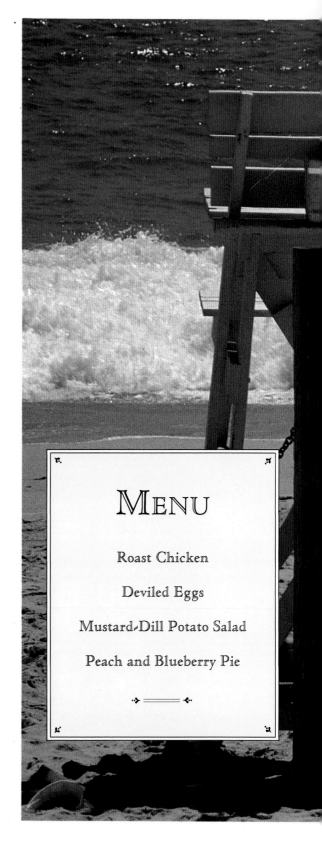

MENU

Roast Chicken

Deviled Eggs

Mustard-Dill Potato Salad

Peach and Blueberry Pie

ROAST CHICKEN

Some of my friends think I'm strange to fire up the oven in July, but roast chicken is too good to pass up just because it's hot. (If it's really a scorcher, I get up early, roast the chicken, and serve it cold later. It's just as good.)

2 chickens, each about 3 pounds, or
   one 5- to 6-pound chicken
Coarse salt
2 garlic cloves
Juice of 2 lemons
Freshly ground pepper

Preheat the oven to 425°F.

Rinse the chickens and pat dry. Sprinkle each inside and out with the coarse salt. Cut the garlic cloves in half and rub the chickens with them. Leave the garlic inside the chickens. Pour the lemon juice over the chickens, inside and out.

Truss the chickens with twine and set on a rack in a roasting pan. Sprinkle with more salt and pepper.

Roast the smaller chickens for 1 hour or 1 hour 15 minutes for the larger chicken, and *do not open the oven* until the cooking time is through. Then test for doneness. The chicken is done when the juices run clear.

Serves 6

. . . .

Terry's convertible converts into a picnic table with a few blankets, opposite. Roast chicken, right, is good hot, cold, or at room temperature on the beach.

Even simple fare tastes best served from real dishes, **above.**

DEVILED EGGS

What would an all-American picnic be without deviled eggs! My favorite is simple, but as good as can be.

6 hard-cooked eggs
½ teaspoon salt
¼ teaspoon pepper
½ teaspoon dry mustard
3 tablespoons mayonnaise
½ teaspoon red wine vinegar
Paprika

Peel the eggs and cut in half lengthwise. Remove the yolks and mash in a small bowl with a fork. Add the salt, pepper, dry mustard, mayonnaise, and vinegar. Mix well.

Mound the yolk mixture into the egg-white halves and garnish with a few shakes of paprika.

Makes 12 deviled eggs

MUSTARD-DILL POTATO SALAD

2 pounds new red potatoes
Salt
½ cup finely chopped celery
⅓ cup finely chopped red onion
2 hard-cooked eggs
½ cup chopped fresh dill
½ cup mayonnaise
1 tablespoon white wine vinegar
1 tablespoon Dijon mustard
Salt and pepper
Lettuce
Cherry tomatoes

Scrub the potatoes and cut into large chunks. Do not peel. Place in a saucepan and cover with salted water. Cover and bring to a boil; reduce the heat and cook until tender, about 15 minutes. Drain and transfer to a bowl. Let cool.

Add the celery, onion, hard-cooked eggs, and dill to the potatoes and toss. Combine the mayonnaise, vinegar, and mustard. Add to the potatoes and toss. Season with salt and pepper to taste.

Serve on a bed of lettuce and garnish with cherry tomatoes.

Serves 6

Deviled eggs, **above,** *are the quintessential picnic food, loved even by those who would rather splash than eat,* **right.**

It's amazing how little advance work has to go into a satisfying and memorable family picnic. The trick is to keep the menu simple and to organize ahead of time. Never forget essential equipment, such as the corkscrew for that bottle of wine, a roll of paper towels, and salt and pepper. My own picnic basket is packed all summer with its own special set of dishes and flatware and plastic glasses. Remember the extra touches—flowers in a jug, a cutting board for a level work surface, baskets that can double as small tables, garbage bags for litter, and a camera loaded with film.

Left and above: *If making a pie crust was a complicated, time-consuming household task, I'd be the first one to come home from the food store with the frozen variety. But the steps are so easy, and the result so unmistakably homemade, I refuse to compromise, especially when I'll be filling the pie shell with fresh fruit from one of our local orchards, opposite.*

BASIC SINGLE PIE CRUST

~

1½ cups sifted all-purpose flour
½ teaspoon salt
½ cup (1 stick) *cold* unsalted
     butter, cut into bits
3 to 4 tablespoons ice water

In a large bowl, mix the flour and salt. Cut in the butter quickly. Add ice water and stir just enough to combine. Form dough into a ball, wrap in wax paper, and refrigerate until ready to use.

Roll out the dough on a floured surface and use as instructed.

Makes 1 9-inch crust

·>——‹·

PEACH AND BLUEBERRY PIE

~

4 cups peeled and sliced ripe
     peaches (6 to 7 peaches)
3 tablespoons sugar
1 tablespoon cornstarch
1 tablespoon lemon juice
1 Basic Single Pie Crust (above)
1 cup fresh blueberries

Preheat the oven to 400°F.

Mix the peaches lightly with 2 tablespoons of the sugar, the cornstarch, and the lemon juice.

Roll out the pie dough and press into a 9-inch pie plate, crimping the edge. Arrange peaches around the sides, leaving the center for the blueberries. Toss the blueberries with the remaining 1 tablespoon sugar. Pour into the center of the filled pie.

Bake for 50 to 60 minutes, or until the pastry is golden and the fruit is soft and bubbly.

Serves 6–8

DAY TRIP FOR TWO

When the kids are underfoot and an otherwise happy season becomes "the long hot summer," it's time to organize a trip on two-wheelers. The best antidote to boredom and lethargy is exercise, I tell Samantha and Jonathan, so "make yourself a picnic and get on those bikes!" It might be a short trip to the beach and back, or a long haul to Montauk or the ferry to Block Island, but they depart with cleverly devised carryalls full of scrumptious fare like cuke sandwiches and salads modeled after the classic soda-fountain sandwich—the BLT. Just when the quiet starts to get overwhelming, they're back with the carryalls full of treasures—wildflowers, bleached bones, driftwood, and even live frogs.

MENU

Lyn Hutching's BLT Salad

Cucumber Sandwiches

Potato Chips

Fresh Fruit

Old-Fashioned Lemonade
(see page 84)

96

AT HOME IN THE COUNTRY

DAY TRIP FOR TWO

Old Ball or Mason jars, once used to "put up" an abundant harvest of fruit or vegetables, can be adapted for countless useful and decorative purposes in the country home: as makeshift but attractive vases (especially good for giving your own home-grown flowers as gifts); as see-through storage jars for nails, pennies, and buttons; or as picnic containers. To add to the jars' antique character, I often paste colorful old seed-packet labels to the sides.

LYN HUTCHING'S
BLT SALAD

Once again Lyn Hutching comes through with a fresh idea for vegetables. I don't know why I didn't think of this myself—I love BLT sandwiches—but ever since Lyn shared it with me, I have it at least once a week in the summertime. The "L" in this mix, by the way, isn't lettuce, but fresh basil leaves.

5 cups cherry tomatoes, halved
6 slices lean bacon, cooked until crisp and crumbled
⅓ cup finely chopped fresh basil leaves
2 tablespoons red wine vinegar
Salt and pepper
¼ cup olive oil, preferably extra-virgin
6 basil sprigs

In a bowl, toss together the tomatoes, bacon, and chopped basil.

In a small bowl, whisk together the vinegar and salt and pepper to taste. Add the oil in a stream and whisk until well blended.

Pour the dressing over the tomato mixture and toss to coat well. Garnish with the basil sprigs.

Serves 6

. . . .

Roadside dining requires ingenuity and appreciation of nature's best, opposite above and below. A simple salad and sandwich are still great picnic companions, right.

102

Country roads, preceding pages and left, and cucumber sandwiches, above.

. . . .

CUCUMBER SANDWICHES

Cucumber sandwiches aren't just something the English munch at teatime; they are a refreshing—and surprisingly filling—meal for a summer road trip. Don't forget the basil (or your own favorite herb). Good as fresh cucumbers are, they can use a zesty companion to boost their flavor.

4 tablespoons mayonnaise	¼ cup chopped fresh basil
6 slices white bread	Coarsely ground black pepper
1 medium cucumber, thinly sliced	

Spread mayonnaise on each slice of bread. Layer on the cucumbers, and then sprinkle with the basil and pepper.

Makes 3 sandwiches

LOBSTER PORCH PARTY

I love lobster so much, I've managed to accumulate over the years a closet full of objects devoted to the noble and tasty crustacean. Lobster dishes, lobster napkins, lobster trays, you name it. I'm well prepared when the time comes to throw a lobster party on my screened porch. It's an inherently messy dinner, but I make it fun for guests by providing huge individual platters that give them plenty of elbow room and sturdy nutcrackers that open the claws in a hurry. For some people summer means hot dogs and ice cream. But for me summer isn't complete without at least one occasion to feast on lobster, corn on the cob, and strawberry shortcake —the classic standbys of August.

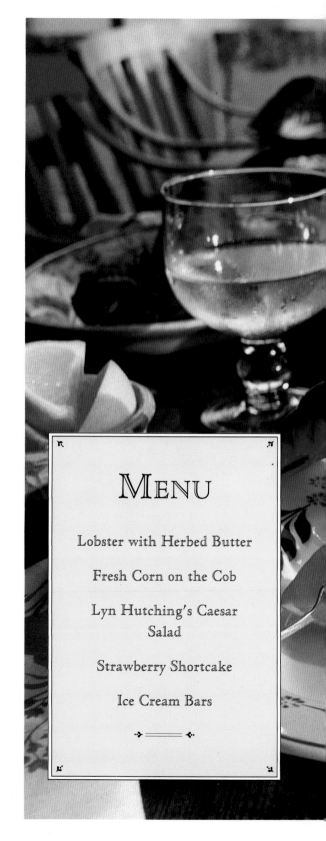

MENU

Lobster with Herbed Butter

Fresh Corn on the Cob

Lyn Hutching's Caesar
Salad

Strawberry Shortcake

Ice Cream Bars

104

LOBSTER WITH HERBED BUTTER

Lobster has to be prepared live, so the least squeamish member of the household should be appointed lobster chef. (Some of my cowardly country friends have actually invited braver guests for the weekend, just so they can enjoy a lobster dinner without having to be present in the kitchen for the critical moment.) Be sure to put empty bowls on the table for discarding shells and claws.

1 live lobster per person, 1 to
   1½ pounds each

Put a large pot of water to boil on the stove. When it has reached a full rolling boil, plunge the lobsters head first into the water and cover the pot. Cook about 5 minutes or until lobsters are bright red. Serve immediately with Herbed Butter (recipe follows).

HERBED BUTTER

2 tablespoons dried herbs (thyme,
   basil, tarragon), or ¼ cup minced
   fresh
½ cup dry white wine
½ cup (1 stick) unsalted butter, at
   room temperature

Combine the herbs and wine in a small bowl. Let sit 2 or more hours.

Melt the butter in a small saucepan over medium heat. Stir in the herb mixture.

Makes about 1 cup

In the age of moderation I like my summer bar to be inviting yet healthful, so I organize it to look its best— as pretty as if it were a dressing table. I fill firkins with small bottles of seltzers and tonics and Classic Cokes. My stirrers and napkins go into heart-shaped wire baskets. Lemons and limes are heaped in a bowl, and crocks serve as olive dishes, ice buckets, and wine coolers.

Every summer place near beach or pool needs quantities of fresh guest towels.

LYN HUTCHING'S CAESAR SALAD

❧

For the croutons:
Olive oil
6 to 8 pieces day-old bread, cut into
    bite-size pieces
Dried oregano to taste

For the dressing:
1 tablespoon coarse salt
Coarsely ground black pepper
2 garlic cloves, crushed and peeled
1 teaspoon Dijon mustard
2 tablespoons red wine vinegar
3 tablespoons olive oil

For the salad:
2 heads romaine lettuce, washed,
    dried, and shredded
2 large eggs, parboiled for
    1½ minutes and set aside
3 tablespoons grated imported
    Parmesan cheese

Caesar salad is a summer favorite.

. . . .

For the croutons: Heat the oil over medium-high heat in a medium skillet. Add the bread cubes and the oregano, reduce the heat to medium, and sauté until lightly toasted, tossing croutons to keep them from burning.

For the dressing: Select the bowl you will use to serve the salad, preferably a large wooden salad bowl. Combine the salt, pepper, and garlic in the bowl. Add the mustard, vinegar, and olive oil and mix briskly until the salt is dissolved.

Add the lettuce to the dressing in the salad bowl and toss to combine. Break the eggs over the salad (they should still be runny) and toss again. Add the Parmesan cheese and the croutons, toss, and serve immediately.

Serves 6

NOTE: If you are concerned about any potential health danger in eating uncooked eggs, you'll have to skip this recipe.

Flowers, left and above, *fill the house at the height of summer.*

STRAWBERRY SHORTCAKE

I dream of this dessert all winter long. Even though strawberries are available for a much longer season than they were when I was growing up, I still think of strawberry shortcake as a summer treat.

2 cups sifted all-purpose flour
1 tablespoon plus 1 teaspoon baking powder
1 tablespoon sugar
¼ cup (½ stick) unsalted butter or vegetable shortening, cut into small bits, plus additional butter to grease pans and spread on cakes
1 large egg
½ cup half-and-half, or ½ cup cream or milk
Melted butter
1 quart fresh strawberries
Sugar
1 cup heavy cream

Preheat the oven to 425°F.

Butter two 8-inch round or square cake pans or a favorite pan.

Sift the flour, baking powder, and sugar into a large bowl. Blend the butter into the flour with a pastry cutter or 2 knives until the mixture resembles coarse cornmeal.

In a small bowl, beat the egg well and stir in the half-and-half. Drizzle the liquid over the flour mixture and stir just enough to combine. If there are still some dry ingredients left in the bowl, drizzle in a little more half-and-half, but only enough so that the dough just holds together when pressed.

Turn the mixture out onto a lightly floured board and shape into a ball, pressing lightly. Avoid over-handling the dough. Cut the ball in half and shape into 2 smaller balls, keeping hands well floured.

Press a ball of dough into each prepared pan. Bake in the middle of the oven for 12 minutes, until tops are golden brown. Turn onto wire racks and brush with butter, about 1 tablespoon on each cake.

While the cakes are baking, wash, dry, and hull the strawberries. Reserve several of the best-looking berries for the top. Slice the remaining berries and crush slightly. Add sugar to taste and set aside. Do not refrigerate. Stir from time to time.

In a medium bowl, whip the cream. Cover the bowl and refrigerate until ready to serve.

To assemble, place one cake on a serving plate and top with half of the crushed berries. Top with the second cake and spoon on the remaining berries. Either spoon on whipped cream or serve it on the side. Decorate with reserved berries.

Serves 6

NOTE: To prepare in advance, prepare pastry and divide into 2 parts. Wrap the balls in aluminum foil and refrigerate. Dough can be prepared up to 8 hours in advance. To bake, leave dough at room temperature for 30 minutes. Then continue by pressing dough into the pans. The berries may also be prepared several hours in advance, but refrigerate after 2 hours.

· ·

Heart shapes, **opposite,** *make the berries even sweeter. Cooking implements stay handy in a crock,* **above.** *Summer ends with sunflowers,* **below.**

· ·

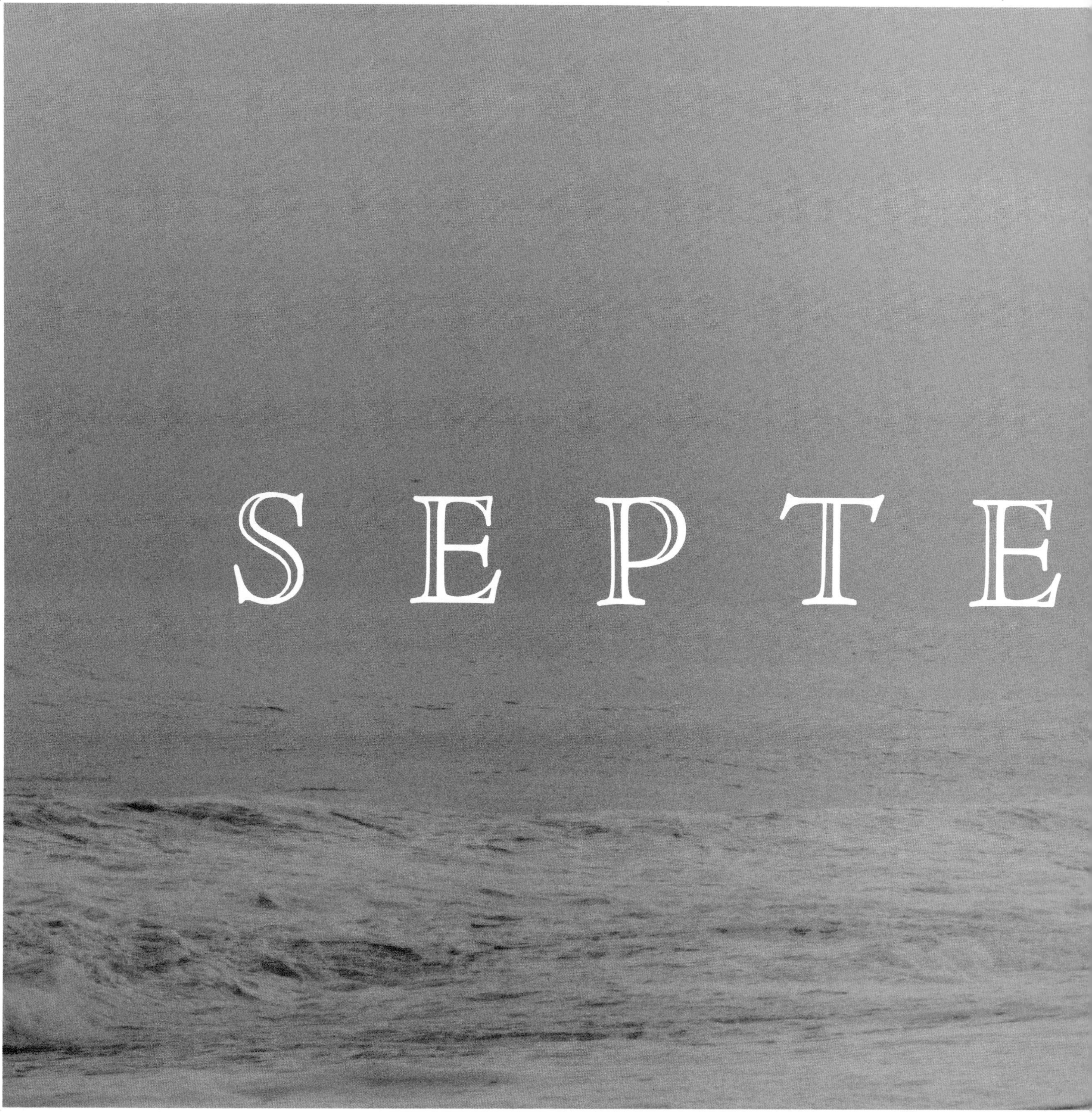
SEPTE

PASTA AL FRESCO

I love September, the month of change, the month when parking spaces suddenly materialize again in front of our general store. It's much too early to retreat indoors, but with the kids in school, our time in the country is mostly limited to weekends, and it's that much more precious. We savor the last tastes of summer, even in a simple pasta dish, with ripe tomatoes from local farms and neighbors' gardens and pungent basil from my own herb patch. (Tomatoes are everywhere at this time of year, so I gave up struggling with my own.) Harvest time is all too short, so we make the most of just-picked fruits and vegetables. The fresh flavors of the season and the solitude of autumn are pleasures we all can share.

MENU

Ziti with Warm Tomato Dressing

Garlic Bread

Arugula, Cantaloupe, and Prosciutto Salad

Lemon Cake with Orange Glaze

114

ZITI WITH WARM TOMATO DRESSING

When local tomatoes are in season, we have them nearly every night. They are wonderful sliced with basil and a bit of olive oil, but this pasta dish with fresh tomatoes is terrific, too. It's even good left over.

¼ cup olive oil
1 dried chili pepper
4 garlic cloves, sliced
1 pound ziti
2 to 3 tablespoons fresh basil or oregano leaves
12 fresh Italian plum tomatoes, seeded and chopped
Salt and coarsely ground pepper
Freshly grated Parmesan cheese

In a small saucepan, heat the oil and chili pepper. When the oil is hot, add the garlic and cook until brown and fragrant. Remove the pan from the heat.

Cook the pasta in rapidly boiling water until tender. Drain. Return the pasta to the pot.

Remove the chili pepper from the oil. Pour the oil and garlic into the pasta and toss. Add the basil and tomatoes, salt and pepper to taste, and toss again.

Serve immediately with lots of Parmesan cheese.

Serves 4

. . . .

An Italian meal is served American style on an outdoor bench, left. Garden pleasures include the antics of a kitten and folk art sculptures, opposite above and below.

GARLIC BREAD

1 long loaf French or Italian bread
½ cup (1 stick) unsalted butter
3 garlic cloves, minced

Preheat the oven to 350°F.

Melt the butter in a small saucepan with the garlic.

Slice the bread, but don't cut all the way down to the bottom. Brush garlic butter into slices and over the top.

Wrap the bread in aluminum foil and warm in the oven until heated through.

Serves 4–6

Exchanging recipes is a gesture of sharing and friendship my mother taught me long ago. I paste or tape recipes into a large three-ring school notebook, divided into sections—Pasta, Appetizers, Salad, etc.—and covered with a remnant of fabric. The vest pocket of the notebook stores recipes I haven't had a chance to test. When I cook from my homemade book, clothespins help me keep it open to the correct page.

LEMON CAKE WITH ORANGE GLAZE

3 cups sugar
1½ cups (3 sticks) unsalted butter or margarine
5 large eggs
3 cups unsifted all-purpose flour
¼ teaspoon salt
1 can (5 ounces) evaporated milk plus water to make 1 cup
2 teaspoons vanilla extract
Grated zest of 1 lemon
½ teaspoon lemon extract

For the orange glaze:
¾ cup orange juice
1 cup sugar
1 tablespoon butter

Beat the sugar and butter in a large bowl until light and fluffy, about 5 minutes. Beat in eggs one at a time; beat well after each addition.

Mix the flour and salt. Alternately add the flour and milk to the large bowl, ending with flour. Fold in the extract and rind. Pour into a greased 10-inch tube pan and bake, starting in a cold oven, at 325°F for 1 hour 45 minutes or until done. Do not open the oven door while the cake is baking.

For the glaze: Put orange juice, sugar, and butter in a saucepan and bring to a boil; boil until it is syrupy, about 45–55 minutes. Then pour glaze over the warm cake slowly, so it seeps in.

Serves 10–12

ARUGULA, CANTALOUPE, AND PROSCIUTTO SALAD

A lot of Americans have adopted the Italian antipasto of melon wrapped in thin slices of prosciutto ham. This recipe uses that sweet-and-salty combination and adds the slightly sour taste of arugula for a cool, delicious late-summer salad.

1 tablespoon white wine vinegar
½ teaspoon grated orange peel
1 tablespoon fresh orange juice
Salt and white pepper
¼ cup olive oil
2 bunches arugula, stems discarded, leaves washed well and spun dry (about 4 cups)
1 small ripe cantaloupe (about 2 pounds), seeds and rind discarded, the flesh cut into ¾-inch pieces and chilled
2 ounces thinly sliced prosciutto ham, cut crosswise into ¼-inch strips

In a small bowl, whisk together the vinegar, orange peel, orange juice, and salt and pepper to taste. Add the oil in a stream and whisk until emulsified.

In a serving bowl, toss the arugula with the dressing until combined well. Arrange on individual plates with the cantaloupe and prosciutto.

Serves 4

. . . .

Arugula, Cantaloupe, and Prosciutto Salad goes well with a glass of Italian red wine, above. Surrounded by roses, Lemon Cake with Orange Glaze makes a presentation piece, right. Fresh from the garden, herbs dominate the flavors of many wonderful summer meals, opposite.

SLEEPOVER PIZZA

Pizza is the one thing I'd like to have with me if I was stranded on a desert island, maybe because it's the fast food I know and love the best. And for once my kids agree with me! When Jonathan has his pals over for a weekend campout (just outside the kitchen door), I let them create their own menus, and pizza is always on their list. I buy balls of fresh pizza dough from a local pizzeria and let the boys loose in the kitchen. Some of their toppings are a little suspect, such as peanut butter with pepperoni, but the kids have a great time, and I'm left free to spend a few hours in antiques stores! Later on they indulge in too much junk food, but at least they start with a meal that's hot and reasonably healthful.

MENU

Pizza

Camp-Out Snacks

120

PIZZA

1 tablespoon olive oil
1¼ cups finely chopped onions
1 garlic clove, minced
1 16-ounce can Italian-style peeled tomatoes
3 tablespoons tomato paste
1 teaspoon dried oregano, crumbled
½ teaspoon sugar
½ teaspoon salt
⅛ teaspoon freshly ground black pepper
Pizza dough from local pizzeria or frozen
Toppings as desired

Heat the oil in a large stainless steel saucepan. Add the onions and garlic and sauté over medium heat, stirring constantly, for 5 minutes.

Puree the tomatoes and their juice in a food processor or break them up with a fork. Add the tomatoes, tomato paste, and seasonings to the saucepan. Bring to a boil, then reduce the heat to low. Cook the sauce, uncovered and stirring occasionally, for 45 minutes to 1 hour, or until thick. Set aside to cool.

If frozen, let the dough thaw.

Preheat the oven to 450°F.

Knead dough lightly, then roll out into a circle slightly larger than the pan. Press into the pan, raising a rim of dough around the edge.

Spoon the sauce onto the dough and spread just to the edge. Add the toppings. Slide the pan into the oven and bake for 15 minutes, or until the edge of the pizza is golden brown and any cheese toppings are melted and browned.

Yields 8 slices

The only tricky part about pizza-making, especially for children, is preparing the dough. So we've arranged with our local pizzeria to buy the dough in single-pizza balls, which we refrigerate (for a few days) or freeze (for months). The pizza tastes authentic and fresh, and the kids don't have to wait for the dough to rise.

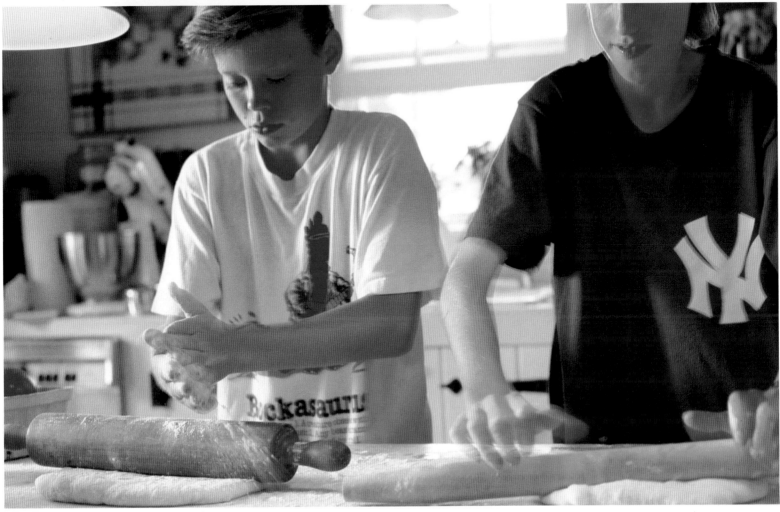

SLEEPOVER PIZZA

123

Jonathan and his friend Nicky enjoy a camping experience safe from the perils of the wild but not the temptations of the supermarket.

OCTO

B E R

CHILI FOR COOL NIGHTS

October is the month for therapeutic activities like baking muffins and cocooning with friends around a big coffee table heaped with books and bowls of chili. The change of seasons is tangibly in the air, and I know it's time to get out the flannel sheets, review all my baking recipes, and prepare the house for winter. It may seem sentimental, but the autumn harvest symbolizes the bounty of America for me. When the roadside stands are brimming with fall vegetables, I can't resist bringing home an armload of pumpkins and gourds—and crisp apples for dessert. To make up for losing our evenings outdoors, I stop by the video store, too, to load up on the makings for an impromptu weekend family film festival.

MENU

Chili à la Mary

Mixed Green Salad with
Balsamic Vinaigrette

Carol Lewis's Onion-Cheese
Muffins

CHILI A LA MARY

1½ pounds boneless sirloin, cut into ¾-inch chunks
1 tablespoon vegetable oil
1 large yellow onion, chopped
1 each yellow, red, and green bell pepper, coarsely chopped
1 to 2 jalapeño peppers, seeded and chopped
2 large garlic cloves, chopped
1 28-ounce can crushed tomatoes
1 6-ounce can tomato paste
1 cup chicken stock
¼ cup minced Mexican chili pepper
1 tablespoon ground cumin
1 teaspoon red pepper flakes
1 teaspoon rubbed sage
¼ to ½ teaspoon cayenne pepper
2 15-ounce cans dark red kidney beans
1 to 2 generous dashes Tabasco, or to taste

In a large skillet, brown the beef and drain.

In a large stockpot, heat the oil over medium-high heat. Add the onion and sauté until translucent. Add the peppers, jalapeño, and garlic; stir well. Add the sirloin, crushed tomatoes, and tomato paste; stir well. Add the chicken stock and spices, and cook over medium heat until the mixture comes to a boil. Reduce the heat to low and simmer until the chili thickens, 20 to 25 minutes.

Rinse the beans well. Add to the chili along with the Tabasco, and return to a boil. Remove from the heat. Let stand, covered, for about 10 minutes.

Serves 6–8

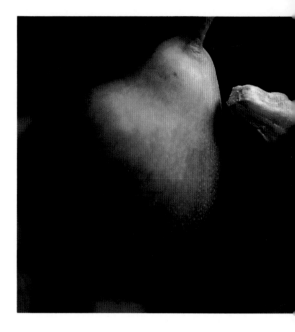

MIXED GREEN SALAD WITH BALSAMIC VINAIGRETTE

2 tablespoons minced shallots
3 tablespoons minced fresh parsley, tarragon, and dill
Coarse salt
2 tablespoons balsamic vinegar
3 tablespoons olive oil, preferably extra-virgin
Mixed salad greens, such as red or green leaf lettuce, Boston lettuce, mâche, watercress, or arugula

In a glass or ceramic bowl, or a blender or food processor, combine the shallots, herbs, salt to taste, and vinegar. Slowly drizzle in the olive oil and beat or process until thoroughly blended.

Let sit at room temperature for about 4 hours.

Wash, dry, and tear mixed salad greens. Add the vinaigrette, toss, and serve.

Serves 8

CAROL LEWIS'S ONION-CHEESE MUFFINS

❧

3 cups Bisquick
¾ cup shredded cheddar cheese
1 7-ounce can french-fried onions
1 large egg
1 cup milk

Preheat the oven to 400°F. Grease a muffin tin.

Combine all the ingredients in a large bowl. Beat for 1 minute.

Fill the muffin cups two-thirds full. Bake for 15 minutes, or until a toothpick inserted in the middle comes out clean.

Serves 4

. . . .

Chili with beans and jalapeños, opposite, fall fruits and nuts, above, and crunchy onion-cheese muffins, right, are ingredients of a savory meal.

GUEST ROOM LUNCH

A weekend in the country always means a flurry of activities, but there's also time for rest and privacy. Fall visitors are always invited to take a "guest room lunch" if they just want to be by themselves for a while, and Many Mushroom Soup is the perfect easy meal to carry from the stove to the bedroom. After a few hours of healing solitude, catnapping, and sampling from the pile of books and magazines I always leave next to the easy chair, my guest invariably emerges refreshed and restored, ready for a game of hearts on the porch, or a long walk on the beach (all bundled up!), and then perhaps a foray into town. We light a fire in the evening and enjoy one another's company again.

MENU

"Wilted" Lettuce

Many Mushroom Soup

"WILTED" LETTUCE

"Wilted" does not usually have a positive meaning, but one taste of this just-warm sweet-and-sour salad will change your impression of the word.

1 large head loose head or leaf lettuce, such as Boston, red leaf, or green leaf
½ cup ham drippings or bacon drippings
½ cup cider vinegar
¼ cup sugar dissolved in 4 tablespoons cold water
2 tablespoons finely chopped red onion
Salt and black pepper

Wash and dry the lettuce; set aside at room temperature.

In a small skillet, cook the drippings over medium heat until smoky. Add the vinegar and sugar; heat for a few more minutes.

Toss the lettuce with the onion and salt and pepper to taste. Pour the dressing over the salad; toss. Serve immediately.

Serves 4

. . . .

An autumn weekend can be bleak or radiant, opposite below, depending on our weather. A well-seasoned "Wilted" Lettuce Salad, left, and robust Many Mushroom Soup, opposite above, suit both extremes, yet can be assembled in a moment.

MANY MUSHROOM SOUP

Soup is the perfect comfort food, and this recipe is my favorite for fall. I don't hunt for wild mushrooms myself, but my friends sometimes do. You shouldn't experiment if you're not an expert, but a lot of supermarkets carry different varieties.

½ cup chopped leeks, white part only

4 tablespoons (½ stick) unsalted butter

½ pound white mushrooms, thinly sliced

½ pound fresh shiitake, chanterelle, or porcini mushrooms, soaked for 5 minutes in ½ cup warm white wine

4 large boiling potatoes, peeled and thinly sliced

4 cups chicken stock

1 to 1½ cups half-and-half

2 cups heavy cream

Salt, pepper, and nutmeg

In a large saucepan, cook the leeks in the butter until tender. Add all the mushrooms with the wine and cook until softened. Add the potatoes and stock, and simmer, covered, until the potatoes are very soft, about 30 minutes.

Cool slightly. Puree in a food processor, then return the soup to a saucepan.

Add the half-and-half, 1 cup of the cream, and seasonings to taste. Heat through; do not boil.

Ladle the soup into bowls and garnish each serving with heavy cream.

Serves 4

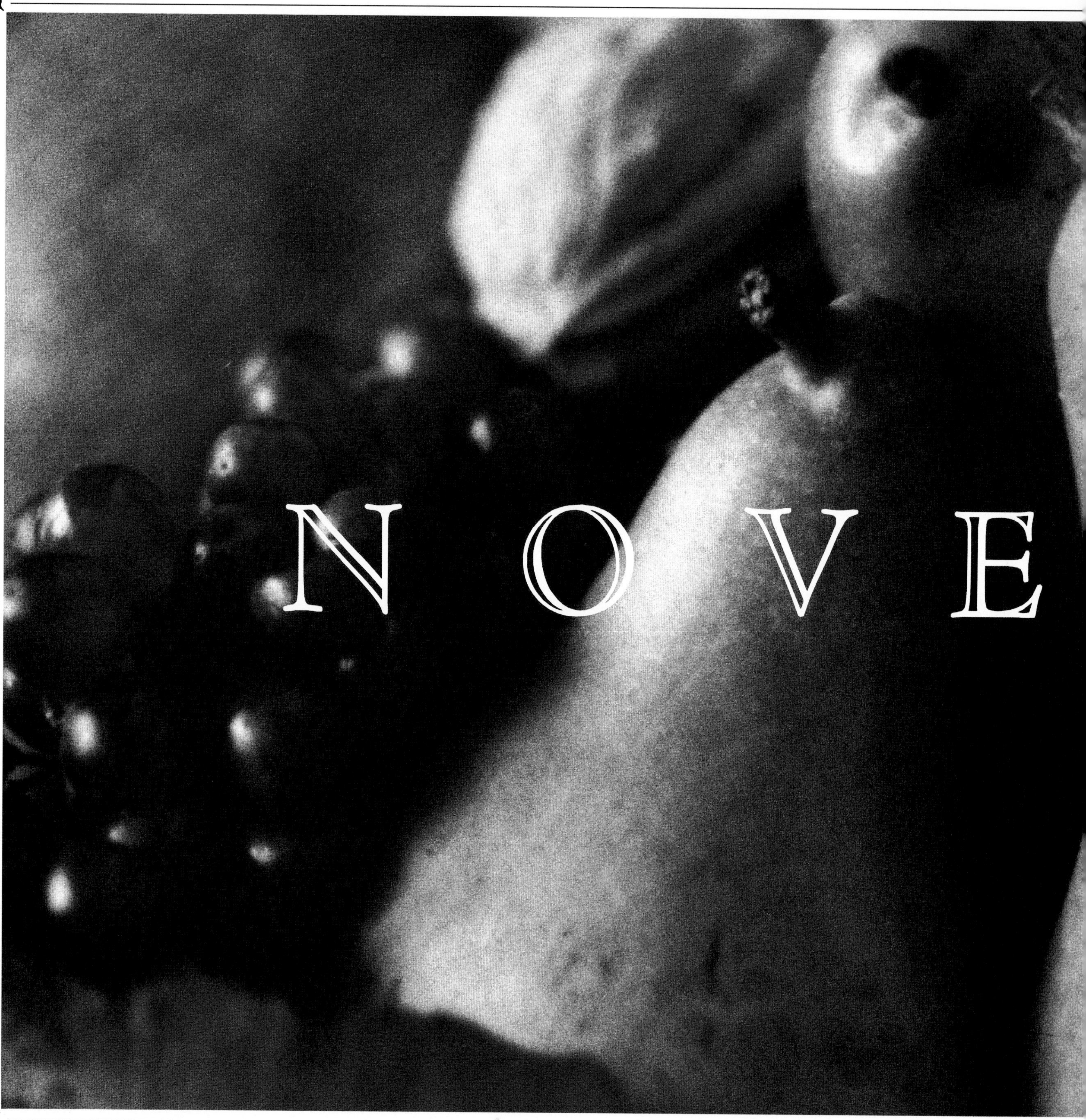
NOVE

M B E R

DAY OF TRADITION

I don't tamper with Thanksgiving Day traditions, because they work! Touch football, old movies, and roast turkey are a combination that leaves everyone in our house with wonderfully corny good feelings. Our champagne toast is the climax of the day for me, and the special turkey plate I prepare for Star is the high point for our dog. The house is dressed for winter now, richer and more festive, with glass candlesticks and gold-rimmed dishes, topiaries and bunches of wildflowers from the countryside, and all the other accoutrements appropriate to a season of celebration. We serve the feast buffet style, because there's so much to heap on one's plate. And everyone pitches in with the dishes when we're done.

MENU

Roast Turkey with
Cornbread Stuffing and
Pan Sauce

Seasonal Vegetables

Cornbread

Emelie Tolley's Marinated
Onions

Sweet Potato Casserole

Raspberry Salad

Tricia Falco's Paper Bag
Apple Pie

Dessert Buffet

ROAST TURKEY WITH CORNBREAD STUFFING AND PAN SAUCE

~

1 12-pound turkey
3 chicken livers
⅓ cup Madeira
About ½ loaf day-old white bread
Cornbread (recipe follows)
½ cup chopped fresh parsley
1 teaspoon dried thyme
Salt and pepper
1 cup (2 sticks) unsalted butter, softened
2 cups minced onions
1 cup chopped celery
2 tablespoons heavy cream
1 small egg
¼ cup plus 1 tablespoon all-purpose flour
1½ cups Turkey Giblet Stock (recipe follows)
⅔ cup light cream

Preheat the oven to 250°F.

Remove and reserve the turkey giblets. Wash the turkey inside and out and dry thoroughly.

Cut the turkey liver and chicken livers into 1-inch pieces. Pour in the Madeira. Set aside.

Cut enough of the white bread into small cubes to measure 3 cups. Toast the cubes in a roasting pan until lightly browned. Set aside. Reset the oven to 325°F.

Crumble enough of the cornbread to measure 7 cups. Place the crumbs in a large bowl; add the bread cubes, parsley, thyme, and salt and pepper to taste. Set aside.

Melt ½ cup (1 stick) of the butter in a large skillet set over medium heat. Add the onions and sauté for 5 minutes. Remove and set aside. Drain the livers, reserving the Ma-

deira, then add to the skillet and sauté until just pink inside. Remove the livers to a blender.

Add the celery to the skillet and sauté for 1 minute. Spoon the celery and onions over the cornbread mixture; toss together.

Place the skillet over high heat and add the reserved Madeira. Cook, scraping the bottom of the pan, until the liquid is reduced to 2 tablespoons. Add the liquid to the blender along with the heavy cream and egg. Blend until completely pureed.

Pour the puree over the bread mixture and combine well. Season with salt and pepper; let cool completely.

Season the turkey inside and out with salt and pepper. Loosely stuff the body and neck cavities with the stuffing. Sew up the openings and truss the bird securely. Coat the bird with the remaining butter.

Put the bird, breast side up, on a rack in a roasting pan. Roast for 3½ to 4 hours, or until a meat thermometer registers 180° to 185°F. If the turkey starts to brown too much, tent loosely with foil. Remove the strings and let the bird rest on a platter for 20 minutes before carving.

To make the pan sauce, discard all but ¼ cup of fat from the roasting pan. Sprinkle on the flour and cook, stirring, over low heat for 2 to 3 minutes. Off the heat, whisk in giblet stock. Return the pan to the heat and bring to a boil. Whisk in the light cream and cook until heated through. Season with salt and pepper to taste. Strain the sauce. Serve in a heated sauceboat.

Serves 8

Ready to be heaped with traditional fare, **opposite,** *the Thanksgiving plate is covered with stars,* **above.**

The original Thanksgiving dinner was undoubtedly more of a buffet than a formal sit-down affair, and that's the way I like it at our house. The sumptuous harvest table laden with all the traditional foods of the season is a dazzling sight. Besides, everyone knows I'm serving turkey, so there's no point in hiding the glorious bird until the last minute.

Arrangements of autumn fruits and nuts decorate the table.

I never refuse help cleaning up in the kitchen. Because of the way I've organized my storage space, it's easy for guests to find their way around. Open shelves make things easy to see and to reach, with pegs and wire racks for towels and utensils, and big crocks and knifeboxes on the countertops for cooking tools and flatware. Tools and dishes are quite good-looking—why not let everyone admire them?

TURKEY GIBLET STOCK

Giblets, neck, and wing tips from a
  fresh turkey
Bouquet garni (1 bay leaf, 1 thyme
  sprig, 12 parsley sprigs, 2 whole
  cloves, tied in a well-washed
  square of cheesecloth)
Fresh celery leaves
1 medium onion, coarsely chopped
1 medium carrot, coarsely chopped
Salt and pepper

Combine the turkey pieces with cold water to cover in a large saucepan. Add the bouquet garni, celery leaves, onion, carrot, and salt and pepper to taste. Bring the water to a boil.

Reduce the heat to low and simmer for at least 1 hour.

Strain the stock, discarding the solids. Keep warm. Reheat when ready to make pan sauce.

Makes about 1 pint

CORNBREAD

1½ cups yellow cornmeal
 1 cup sifted all-purpose flour
 1 tablespoon baking powder
1¼ teaspoons salt
 ¾ cup (1½ sticks) unsalted butter,
    melted and cooled
 2 large eggs, lightly beaten
1½ cups milk

Preheat the oven to 375°F.
Butter a 9-inch square pan.
In a mixing bowl, sift together the cornmeal, flour, baking powder, and salt. Add the butter, eggs, and milk and stir until just combined.

Pour the batter into the prepared pan. Bake for 40 to 45 minutes or until golden. Cool in the pan.

Makes about 8 cups crumbled corn-bread

EMELIE TOLLEY'S MARINATED ONIONS

1 pound pickling onions (pearl
    onions)
Salt
1 quart water, heated to boiling
2 cups white wine vinegar
1 tablespoon light brown sugar
1 tablespoon pickling spice

Cut the tops and bottoms off the onions, leaving the rest of the skin intact. Put the onions in a deep bowl. Dissolve the salt in boiling water and let cool. Pour half the brine over the onions. Leave to pickle for 24 hours.

Remove the onions from the bowl, peel, and return to the bowl with the remaining brine to cover. Weight down the onions with a heavy plate and leave to pickle again for another 48 hours.

Prepare canning jars according to manufacturer's instructions.

In a large saucepan, bring the vinegar, brown sugar, and pickling spice to a boil. Reduce the heat and simmer gently for 5 minutes. Lift the onions from the bowl, discarding the brine, and pack into canning jars. Pour spiced vinegar over onions, seal the jars as directed, and store until needed.

Makes approximately 1 pint

SWEET POTATO CASEROLE

6 medium sweet potatoes, trimmed
   and boiled until tender
4 tablespoons (½ stick) unsalted
   butter, softened
¼ teaspoon ground cinnamon
¼ teaspoon ground mace
⅓ cup heavy cream
⅓ to ½ cup cognac
Salt
Butter
½ cup finely chopped almonds or
   miniature marshmallows
   (optional)

Preheat the oven to 375°F.

Puree the sweet potatoes in a food processor or through a food mill. Stir in the softened butter, cinnamon, mace, and cream. Whisk in the cognac. Season with salt to taste.

Spoon the mixture into a casserole. Dot with butter and sprinkle with almonds or marshmallows.

Bake for 35 minutes or until browned.

Serves 8

. . . .

Thanksgiving plates need to be big enough to hold a bit of every dish on the table—two or three vegetables (such as beans and Brussels sprouts), sweet potatoes, marinated onions, and my favorite Southern treat, cornbread stuffing.

RASPBERRY SALAD

2 10-ounce packages frozen
 raspberries
2 6-ounce packages or 1 12-ounce
 package raspberry Jell-O
1 20-ounce can crushed pineapple
 in syrup
2½ cups liquid: 1½ cups boiling
 water and juice from frozen
 raspberries
1 cup sour cream, plus additional
 for garnish

Defrost the frozen raspberry bags
in hot water. Strain the berries; reserve the juice.

Mix the Jell-O and crushed pineapple with liquid, Add the raspberries. Stir in the sour cream.

Pour into 10-inch mold and put
in the refrigerator overnight.

When ready to serve, put mold
in pan of hot water for a second.
Turn over onto plate. Garnish with
additional sour cream.

Serves 8

*Dessert is more satisfying after
a turn at the kitchen sink,
opposite. Raspberry salad, above,
is a refreshing switch from
the usual greens—and it can be
made ahead of time.*

TRICIA FALCO'S PAPER BAG APPLE PIE

*The paper bag keeps the pie's edges
from overbrowning without the fuss
of aluminum foil.*

1 Basic Single Pie Crust (page 93)
About 2½ pounds apples, preferably
 Granny Smith
1 cup sugar
2 tablespoons plus ½ cup sifted
 all-purpose flour
½ teaspoon ground nutmeg
2 tablespoons lemon juice
½ cup (1 stick) unsalted butter, in
 pieces

Preheat oven to 425°F.

Line pie pan with pastry.

Pare, core, and quarter the apples. Halve each quarter crosswise
to make chunks; place in a large
bowl.

Combine ½ cup of the sugar, 2
tablespoons of the flour, and the nutmeg in a cup. Sprinkle over the apples; toss. Spoon the apples into the
shell and drizzle with lemon juice.

Combine the remaining ½ cup
sugar and ½ cup flour in a small
bowl. Cut in the butter and blend
until mixture is a large crumble.
Sprinkle the topping over the apples.

Slide the pie into a heavy brown
paper bag large enough to hold the
pie loosely. Fold the open end over
twice and fasten securely (I use sta-
ples). Place on a large baking sheet.

Bake for 1 hour, or until the apples are tender and the top is bubbly
and golden. Split the bag open, remove the pie, and set aside to cool
on a wire rack.

Serves 8

MBER

JOYS OF CHRISTMAS

All year long I think about Christmas, and I try to do most of my shopping long before December rolls around. But the spirit of the holiday doesn't really take hold until family rituals begin, such as our visit to the Christmas tree farm. It's when the rooms of the house twinkle with votive candles and the air is heady with the scents of our tree and of the narcissus, forced to bloom in some of my old bowls, that I know the celebration is at hand. Our Long Island roast Duck with Onion and Ginger Marmalade is the equivalent of Tiny Tim Cratchit's Christmas goose. I try to use my keepsakes to make the Christmas table so warm and inviting that someone might be inspired to declare, "God bless us everyone!"

MENU

Hot Parmesan Puffs

Cream Cheese in
Mushrooms

Duck with Onion and
Ginger Marmalade

Susan Victoria's Frozen
Orange Soufflé

Christmas Cookies

Sugar Cookies

Devil's Food Cake with
Crème Anglaise

Chocolate Nut Truffles

Mulled Cider with Apples
and Cloves

Champagne

Christmas is too special to wait until after Thanksgiving to think about it, and I want to enjoy myself, not rush all over making last-minute preparations. Everywhere I travel I have my gift list in mind. I gather tree trimmings and order the tree in advance, and rely on tried and true recipes for Christmas dinner. That way I can concentrate on decking the house in its seasonal finery and taking care of the other little extras that mean so much to family and friends.

HOT PARMESAN PUFFS

These melt-in-your-mouth delights should be served as soon as they emerge from the oven. We usually don't make it past the kitchen door with the serving tray.

1 3-ounce package cream cheese, at room temperature
1 cup mayonnaise
1½ teaspoons grated onion
⅓ cup grated Parmesan cheese
⅛ teaspoon cayenne pepper
1 loaf thin-sliced bread
Grated Parmesan cheese
Paprika

Preheat the oven to 300°F.
In a bowl, mix the cream cheese, mayonnaise, onion, Parmesan, and cayenne. (You can do this in advance.)
Cut 2-inch bread rounds with a cookie cutter or a small glass. Bake on a cookie sheet for 5 minutes, until hardened.
Spread the cheese mixture generously on one side of each bread round. Sprinkle with grated Parmesan cheese and a dash of paprika. Broil until puffy and golden on top, about 5 to 7 minutes. Serve hot.

Makes 30 puffs

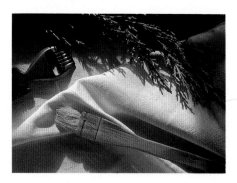

CREAM CHEESE IN MUSHROOMS

½ pound white mushrooms
1 8-ounce package cream cheese, softened
3 to 4 tablespoons chopped scallions
1 tablespoon commercial seasoned salt

Preheat the oven to 375°F.
Wash and scoop out the mushrooms.
Mix all ingredients in a bowl, then fill mushrooms with mixture.
Bake for 15 to 20 minutes.

Makes about 12 mushrooms

. . . .

Light but delectable appetizers, **above left and right,** *presented in assorted trays and bowls along with traditional greenery,* **left,** *establish a festive atmosphere.*

DUCK WITH ONION AND GINGER MARMALADE

Duckling is a Long Island specialty and perfect for a special occasion.

2 Muscovy ducks (each 2 to
   3 pounds)
Salt and pepper

For the marmalade:
¼ cup clarified butter
2 large onions, thinly sliced
2 tablespoons grated fresh ginger
3 tablespoons honey
2 tablespoons candied ginger,
   finely julienned

Preheat the oven to 250°F.

Remove the thighs and legs from the ducks; reserve for another use. Wash the ducks and dry with paper towels. Sprinkle inside and out with salt and pepper. Lightly prick the skin to allow the fat to escape.

Place on a rack in a foil-lined roasting pan and roast for 2 hours. Remove from the oven to cool.

For the marmalade: Melt the butter in a small saucepan over low heat. Add the onions and cook until just translucent. Add the remaining ingredients, raise the heat, and boil for several minutes until the mixture thickens. Set aside to cool slightly.

As soon as the duck is cool enough, skin and bone the breast. Heat some of the rendered fat in a large skillet and quickly brown the breasts.

Slice the breasts into medium medallions and serve with Onion and Ginger Marmalade.

Serves 6

Scents of freshly made
potpourri and a warming
mug of cider from a pot we
keep simmering on the stove
welcome visitors at
Christmastime. More than at
any other time of year,
country guests need
pampering during the
holidays. Our holiday visitors
find fresh flowers, new
magazines, good books, and
candles in their rooms, and
the guest bathroom offers an
array of soaps, lotions, and
all the other comforts I
appreciate having when I am
on the road myself.

Oranges studded with cloves, above,
and hot spiced cider scent the house.

SUSAN VICTORIA'S FROZEN ORANGE SOUFFLÉ

Although it's almost embarrassingly easy to prepare, this orange soufflé from my friend Susan always makes a big impression. With all the rich desserts on the Christmas groaning board, the fresh cool taste of the oranges makes a good contrast.

 4 large oranges
Yolks of 6 large eggs
 ¾ cup sugar
2¾ cups heavy cream, whipped
 ¾ cup Grand Marnier
Grated zest of 1 orange
Cocoa (optional)

Cut oranges in half; scoop out pulp and reserve for another use.

Combine egg yolks and sugar in a medium bowl and beat until stiff. Fold 2 cups of whipped cream into the yolk mixture, then fold in the Grand Marnier. Add the grated rind. Fill orange cups with mixture and freeze for at least 2 hours or preferably overnight.

To serve, top with remaining whipped cream. Sprinkle with cocoa if desired.

Serves 8

. . . .

A miniature log house amid a forest of topiary herbs symbolizes the holiday season of America's pioneer past, when the whole family spent long winter evenings before the fire. I often fill a bowl with ornaments, as well as hanging them on the tree.

Homemade Christmas cookies are worth producing in double and triple batches—they make small gifts for neighbors, mail carriers, and anyone else who might stop by.

CHRISTMAS COOKIES

For families, Christmas cookies are an essential ingredient for enjoying and sharing the holidays. Get the kids to help cut out and decorate the cookies, and pierce holes in a few to string and hang on the tree.

For the dough:
    1 pound (4 sticks) unsalted
       butter, at room temperature
    1 cup granulated sugar
    1 large egg
    2 teaspoons vanilla extract
    4½ cups sifted all-purpose flour

For the icing:
    2 egg whites
    ¼ teaspoon cream of tartar
Pinch of salt
    2 teaspoons vanilla extract
    3 cups confectioners' sugar
Food coloring
Sprinkles and colored sugar

For the dough: With an electric mixer, cream the butter and the granulated sugar. Add the egg and vanilla and gradually beat in the flour, scraping down the sides of the bowl as necessary.

Divide the dough into 4 equal parts. Wrap each in plastic and refrigerate for 2 hours.

Preheat the oven to 375°F. Lightly grease 2 baking sheets.

One at a time, roll out each portion of dough ⅛ inch thick. Cut out cookies with decorative cutters and place on the prepared baking sheets.

Bake for 6 to 9 minutes, until lightly browned. Remove the cookies to cool on a wire rack.

For the icing: Beat the egg whites, cream of tartar, and salt until stiff. Beat in the vanilla. Gradually beat in the confectioners' sugar until the mixture is stiff.

Divide the icing among 5 bowls and color as desired.

Use a pastry tube or toothpick to decorate cookies. Sprinkle with sprinkles and colored sugar.

Makes 24 cookies

SUGAR COOKIES

    1 cup unsifted all-purpose flour
    2 cups sifted bread flour
    1 teaspoon baking powder
    ¼ teaspoon salt
    ½ cup (1 stick) unsalted butter
    1 cup sugar
    1 large egg
    1 teaspoon vanilla extract or grated
       lemon or orange zest
    ⅓ cup sour cream

Preheat the oven to 400°F.

Sift together the dry ingredients.

Beat the butter and sugar until creamy. Beat in the egg. Add the vanilla or grated rind. Add the sour cream.

Fold the dry ingredients into the butter mixture. Wrap in wax paper and refrigerate for at least 1 hour.

On a lightly floured board, roll out one-third of the cookie dough at a time. Roll to about ⅛ inch thick and cut with your favorite cookie cutters (antique or new). Space cookies about ½ inch apart on buttered baking sheets and bake for 10 minutes until lightly colored but not brown. Cool on racks.

Makes 12 cookies

DEVIL'S FOOD CAKE WITH CRÈME ANGLAISE

8 ounces semisweet chocolate
1 cup (2 sticks) unsalted butter
¼ cup heavy cream
5 large eggs, separated
¼ cup sugar
1 cup sifted cake flour

For the crème anglaise:
4 egg yolks
3 tablespoons sugar
2 cups half-and-half
½ vanilla bean

Preheat the oven to 325°F. Butter and flour a 10-inch round cake pan or antique mold.

In a double boiler, melt the chocolate and butter together over simmering water. Stir in the cream.

In a separate bowl, beat the egg whites until they form stiff peaks. Carefully fold, do not stir, about one-quarter of the egg whites into the chocolate mixture. Fold in the remaining egg whites.

In an electric mixer at medium speed, beat the egg yolks with the sugar until thickened and light. Carefully fold in the chocolate mixture by hand. Slowly add the flour and fold in.

Pour the batter into the prepared pan and bake for 45 to 50 minutes, or until a toothpick inserted in the center tests clean. Cool in the pan for 5 minutes and then invert onto a rack to finish cooling.

For the crème anglaise: Whisk together the egg yolks and 2 tablespoons of the sugar until smooth.

Scald the half-and-half with the remaining 1 tablespoon sugar and the vanilla bean.

Stir one-third of the scalded cream into the yolk mixture to warm it. Pour the yolk mixture into the pan. Stir over low heat until the mixture thickens slightly. Do not let boil. Remove the vanilla bean.

Chill the sauce, covered.

To serve, pour the crème anglaise around the base of the cake. Garnish with fresh mint leaves.

Serves 8–10

CHOCOLATE NUT TRUFFLES

9 ounces bittersweet or semisweet chocolate, broken into small pieces
⅔ cup heavy cream
4 tablespoons (½ stick) unsalted butter
1 teaspoon vanilla extract
¾ cup chopped pistachios, walnuts, pecans, almonds, or hazelnuts

In a medium saucepan, combine the chocolate, cream, butter, and vanilla. Cook over low heat until the chocolate melts. Remove from the heat and whisk until smooth.

Pour into a shallow bowl. Press plastic wrap directly onto the surface of the chocolate. Refrigerate overnight or for several days to allow chocolate to harden.

Using a teaspoon, scoop out chocolate and roll with hands to form 1-inch balls. Roll in the chopped nuts, coating completely. Place on wax paper.

Refrigerate the truffles, covered, for up to 1 week, or freeze airtight for up to 1 month. Remove from freezer 5 minutes before serving.

Makes 36 truffles

Surrounded by crème anglaise, Devil's Food Cake is an elegant dessert to end the most important dinner of a year of country weekends.

Baking has an almost magical capacity to bring a family together. The aromas wafting from the oven cast a spell on all of us, no matter where we are in the house or what we are doing. Cookies, cakes, and pies fairly stream out of my kitchen in December, with friends and relatives involved in the preparations as well as the eating.

ACKNOWLEDGMENTS

I have spent lots of wonderful days and nights entertaining and being entertained with friends and their friends. Many friends have shared their favorite recipes with me. Their friendships and lovely evenings and weekends at my house or theirs gave me my personal recipe notebook. I'm happy to share these recipes and times with you.

Gayle Benderoff and Deborah Geltman, my agents, have my warm and always grateful thanks for their enthusiasm and involvement on each and every project.

I will be forever grateful for the humor and love (and always, Mother's Day Breakfast) of my children Jonathan and Samantha.

A big thanks to Joshua Greene, whose love of photography shows in this beautiful book, and who introduced me to Kevin Crafts, for whose work on the food and menus I will be thankful forever.

To Chris Mead, who for the last twelve years has taught me the fun of entertaining and has offered suggestions and encouragement in every part of my day.

To Carol Sama Sheehan and Larry Sheehan, who should be my biographers—they do know me the best and always make my words flow.

To my designer Gina Davis, who made *all* our work look good.

Special thanks go to Lauren Shakely, my editor, for always grasping the concept of my books, from the beginning. And to all involved in all my books at Clarkson Potter and Crown Publishers: Catherine Sustana; Howard Klein; Carol Southern; Bruce Harris; Amy Schuler; Laurie Stark; Michelle Sidrane; Phyllis Fleiss; Jo Fagan; Jonathan Fox; Cameron Dougan; Barbara Marks; Mark McCauslin; Joan Denman; Hilary Bass in Publicity, who is always there for me; and Gail Shanks and everyone else on the sales force.

Have fun at home—cooking and entertaining all during the year.

Mary Emmerling
Sagaponack, Long Island

I N D E X